Airspeed, Altitude, and a Sense of Humor

The Adventures of a Jet Tanker Pilot

Ronnie Ridley George

Captain, USAF

EAKIN PRESS ⨂ Austin, Texas

FIRST EDITION
Copyright © 2001
By Ronnie Ridley George
Published in the United States of America
By Eakin Press
A Division of Sunbelt Media, Inc.
P.O. Drawer 90159 ▣ Austin, Texas 78709-0159
email: eakinpub@sig.net
▣ website: www.eakinpress.com ▣

ALL RIGHTS RESERVED.

1 2 3 4 5 6 7 8 9

1-57168-497-2

For CIP information, please access:
www.loc.gov

This book is dedicated to:

My loving wife and best friend, Barbara,
who thought this book was kinda silly
but still helped me with the project,
and
My son Jim, who said, "Dad, I thought you
were supposed to be famous before you
wrote a book,"
and
My son Robert, who said, "Dad, that's not
the way you told the story last time."

Contents

FOREWORD

Military flying in general, and combat flying in particular, often involves intense experiences that are difficult to forget. I have discovered, however, since I have joined the Medicare Generation, my "forgetter" is more efficient than my memory. In spite of this failing, reading Ronnie's account of our shared experiences has revived a flood of memories of those days. (Yes, I know he usually goes by "Ron" today, but back when we were the pilot team on SAC Crew R-112, he was just a young kid to me, and he will always be "Ronnie" to me.)

Ronnie relates some of our shared experiences in extraordinary detail, some of which I remember and some I had forgotten. Either he kept a diary (which I have often wished I had done), or he has a far better memory than I. Or maybe he just has a younger memory! At any rate, Ronnie has done a fine job of recapturing the flavor of those days.

As Charles Dickens said, "It was the best of times; it was the worst of times." Military men have a love-hate relationship with war. They spend decades and sometimes careers preparing for combat which they hope will never come. When it does come, however, there is a feeling of satisfaction of a job well done. The shared experiences of a crew flying in combat build a camaraderie that is hard to equal in civilian life. At the same time, the military man realizes the suffering that war causes, and he hates it. And he hates being absent from home and loved ones for many months at a time.

Someone once described flying as "hours of boredom interspersed with moments of stark terror." That might also describe the life of a SAC combat crewmember during the worst days of the Cold War.

The boredom was the alert duty, days and sometimes weeks at a time, separated from home and family and with little to do to pass the time. For me, the terror was the occasional landings I had to attempt. So much of our time was spent on alert duty that we seldom got a chance to do much flying. And there were the crosswinds. The KC-135 was a little difficult to land in a crosswind, and most of my "arrivals" in those days were in West Texas, at either El Paso or Abilene, where high crosswinds were a constant fact of life.

It was rumored that when SAC planners were surveying for a new base, they carefully studied the prevailing winds and built the runways exactly perpendicular to them. At any rate, I never became comfortable landing the 135 until my first combat tour in Southeast Asia in 1967 where we flew at least once a day and sometimes more. After that, I never again sweated a landing in the 135.

When Ronnie speaks of the KC-135, he is referring to the "A model," the "water wagon," that ground-loving son-of-a-gun with water-injection engines that produced heart-stopping takeoff rolls which only ended when the pilot pulled it off the ground at the end of the runway. We didn't have the luxury of the souped-up version with fan-jet engines flown by today's pilots.

After retiring from the Air Force in 1978, I did some charter flying in light Cessnas in California. I used to brag to the young pilots that I had more time on takeoff roll than they had in total flight time. Only an old KC-135 airman could appreciate how close to the truth that was.

I believe reading Ronnie's account of his experiences will be an enjoyable experience for anyone interested in flying, but especially for other old SAC pilots like me who like to swap war stories about the old days.

DARRELL R. DUNLOP
Major, USAF, Retired

PREFACE

In his article "Tribute to the Tankers," published in the January 1996 issue of *Air Force* magazine, contributing editor John L. Frisbee noted that in the Southeast Asia war, air refueling became, for the first time, a key element in combat operations. Between 1965 and 1973, he reported, Strategic Air Command tankers in Southeast Asia "flew about 195,000 sorties, made nearly 814,000 refuelings, and offloaded almost nine billion pounds of fuel. That war, with its military achievements and political handicaps, could not have been fought without them."

This book, *Airspeed, Altitude, and a Sense of Humor,* is part of a larger, unpublished manuscript entitled "As I Recall," which I originally wrote for my friends and family about my adventures as an Air Force pilot, as the son of a railroad fireman, as a farm boy growing up in Texas, later years as a wildlife biologist, and other things. I should have kept a journal, but I didn't.

These are my stories, as I recall them, about flying—beginning with my earliest memories of airplanes, my own first solos, aerobatics, supersonic flight, squadron life, alert duty, combat missions, and gas stations high in the sky over Texas, Alaska, Greenland, and Southeast Asia.

Acknowledgments

I gratefully acknowledge the assistance of all of those who waded through early drafts of this book and provided valuable comments. I am especially grateful to former U. S. Air Force pilots Darrell Dunlop, Jack Bauer, and Mike George (my younger brother), who reviewed the technical portions of the book. Air Force instructor pilot James Finfinger assisted with airspeeds. Air Force weapons system operator Phil Zwank shared his Vietnam-era list of air refueling tracks and radio frequencies. Air Force pilot training classmates Robert Kusterer and John Cantwell; M/Sgt. Robert T. Romanelli, Dyess Air Force Base; Susan Lewis, Hangar 25, Webb AFB; Oscar Lopez, Texas Parks and Wildlife; and Dave Miller, Texas State Aircraft Pooling Board, assisted with photographs. My mom, Dorris Ridley George (now deceased); my older brother Larry George; my cousin Bill Fleming; my friend and best man, Fred Bennett, Jr.; and my Iowa friends, Gay and Lloyd Crim, and Lloyd's mother, Mildred Crim, provided valuable insights. I am very grateful to Texas Parks and Wildlife coworkers Bob Cook, Mike Berger, David Mabie, Don Wilson, Bill Harvey, Rollin MacRae, Gene Miller, and Lydia Saldana, who offered their thoughts and encouragement. John Foshee assisted with song titles and lyrics, and Lisa Engeling assisted with editing.

CHAPTER 1

AIRPLANES

"Off we go into the wild blue yonder,
climbing high into the sun!"
"The Army Air Corps Song"
Maj. Robert Crawford, 1939

In February 1968 we were flying an unarmed aircraft along the Laotian border somewhere west of Hanoi when a clear, dispassionate, monotone voice on emergency Guard Channel calmly announced, "Bandits . . . Bandits . . . Airborne . . . Phuc . . . Yen . . . Climbing . . . 10 Angels . . . Turning . . . 2 . . . 7 . . . 0." This voice was coming from an Air Force EC-121 Super Constellation radar aircraft flying "MiG Watch" over the Gulf of Tonkin. It was warning U.S. aircraft that Russian-built North Vietnamese MiG fighters (bandits) had just taken off from Phuc Yen Air Base near Hanoi and were climbing through 10,000 feet and turning west to intercept American aircraft. As I tell you this story thirty years later, in the safety of my own home, the hair still stands up on the back of my neck.

They say some pilots are born to fly, but I don't think I was one of them. As a boy, my kites wouldn't fly and my paper airplanes crashed. Some of my school classmates built a lot of model airplanes from kits, but I recall putting together only one model airplane. It was a Korean War-era U.S. Navy "Panther" jet, which I made out of thin balsa wood strips and then covered with waxy tissue paper. I painted it black. It lasted until my friend Don Rutland tried to test fly it and broke off a wing. The possibility I might actually fly an airplane never occurred to me.

1

We were living in Commerce, Texas, in the late 1940s and early '50s on a direct line between Texarkana and the Dallas-Fort Worth area. We saw a lot of airplane traffic: light planes, commercial airliners, and military stuff, but a few stand out in my memory.

A really remarkable plane we saw in those years was the huge, swept-wing, B-36 bomber with six pusher props. The B-36s were coming out of Carswell Air Force Base at Fort Worth, 100 miles to the west. By the time they passed Commerce, they were still relatively low (maybe 20,000 feet), climbing at full military power, and dragging white contrails across a winter sky. Their powerful engines set up some sort of harmonic which made the ground seem to tremble. B-36s were incredible airplanes, but they were rendered obsolete in only a few years by jets.

One day I was playing in the big canvas-shaded sandbox in the backyard on Ash Street when I heard a tremendous roar directly overhead. When I looked out from under the sunshade, I saw a sleek, swept-wing jet fighter, flying no more than 200 feet off the deck and rapidly disappearing to the east. I knew instantly it was a "Sabre Jet." The Korean War was in full swing, and we had been hearing a lot about this new fighter. The pilot of the aircraft was probably a former college student who came back to buzz the town. That F-86 was the first jet fighter I had ever seen.

About 1953, we began to hear sonic booms in Commerce from the passage of supersonic aircraft. The boom sounded just like an explosion, and everyone was trying to figure out what had blown up until Mom heard on radio station KGVL in Greenville what was really happening. Every few days, and sometimes several times a day, we would get another sonic boom. When you heard a boom, it was often difficult to locate the aircraft in the sky because the aircraft was traveling faster than its sound. When the aircraft was at high altitude, there was often just a contrail to show where it had been.

That same year, I was looking out the front window of the Safeway grocery store in Commerce when a sonic boom hit. The huge plate-glass window bowed inward and nearly touched a steel support column mounted a good six inches in from the glass. If the glass had hit the column and broken, I might not be writing this because I was standing right where it would have fallen. Public complaints about the noise and property damage from the sonic booms eventually forced the military to restrict supersonic flights to less populated areas and higher altitudes.

My only close-up encounter with a real airplane in those early years was at a grade-school field trip to the Commerce airport. Our teachers marched us up to one door of a low-winged light plane (possibly a Piper Cherokee), and told us to slide across the seats and exit out the other door. We were not allowed to touch anything, and I don't recall anyone explaining anything about the airplane. The cabin looked like the inside of an automobile. I was not impressed.

CHAPTER 2

First Flight

"Oh, I have slipped the surly bonds of Earth
and danced the skies on laughter silvered wings."
From the poem "High Flight"
Maj. John Gillespie Magee, Jr.

I probably didn't think a lot more about flying until I started college at East Texas State in Commerce in 1961. My older brother, Larry, had enrolled in the Air Force Reserve Officers Training Corps (AFROTC), so I did too. It was like playing soldier; we wore uniforms to class on Mondays and marched around and saluted the older cadets. There were less than 100 cadets in the entire Cadet Corps, and I felt self-conscious wearing my uniform since I was often the only one dressed like that in many of my classes.

Six real Air Force personnel (three officers and three sergeants) ran the ROTC unit. Some of the officers were combat veterans of the Korean War with impressive silver wings and rows of ribbons on their blue uniforms. Captain Toedt had flown P-51 Mustangs, and Captain Koeller had flown F-84 Thunderstreaks in Korea. The influence of those men and about two years of marching and classroom training brought me to a major crossroad in my life.

Out of the blue one day, Major Farrell, the detachment commander, called me into his office and told me I had passed the written flight aptitude test and physical exam necessary for Air Force pilot training. I was dumbfounded; flying was some-

4

thing other people like Major Farrell did, not me! I was scared of heights! I got queasy looking out the seventh-floor window of the Greenville National Bank Building. Major Farrell must have sensed I was uncomfortable because he began to tell me what a wonderful opportunity this was. He said that to him, flying an airplane was like playing baseball; flying was so much fun he would do it even if no one paid him. He also said I didn't have to make a final decision right away, but he would go ahead and process the preliminary paperwork. What he didn't tell me was that there would be no graceful way out.

A few months later, Major Farrell and Captain Toedt took several of us promising birdmen to Perrin Air Force Base, near Sherman on the Red River, for some flight indoctrination. After being fitted with flight suits and given survival and flight brief-ings, we were taken out to the flight line and given a ride in the back of an H-43 "Huskie" Air Rescue helicopter. The local Air Rescue personnel planned to take us only up to 500 feet, so we weren't issued parachutes. They said at that height the chutes wouldn't open anyway, so why bother wearing them? That was certainly a comforting thought!

The H-43 shook as though it would come apart at any moment from engine start, up to 500 feet, and back to the ground. I had had my first aircraft flight, but I knew from that moment on helicopters were not my bag.

After the helicopter flight, we were taken to the Perrin Mess Hall and introduced to that famous Air Force mess hall staple, wieners and beans. Then it was back to the flight line for a ride in the back seat of a Lockheed T-33 "T-Bird," a single-engine jet trainer. Captain Toedt and a crew chief helped me get strapped in. This time, there was a parachute along with a confusing array of lap belts, shoulder harness, oxygen hoses, and electrical wires. Captain Toedt warned me to keep my hands away from the ejection seat handles unless he hollered "Bail out!" and to keep my fingers away from the red button on the instrument panel because it would jettison our wingtip fuel tanks. He then climbed into the front seat, completed his checklist, asked me through the intercom if I could hear him okay, and started the jet engine. I assumed the garbled noises coming from the radio had something to do with clearance from the Perrin Control

Tower because we left the parking ramp, taxied out, and began to accelerate down the runway. The T-33 was fast on takeoff but did not have the "take your breath away" acceleration I had imagined for a jet aircraft. Once airborne, I noticed I still seemed to be sitting on something solid, not floating through the air like I had expected, or shaking like the helicopter; this was a pleasant surprise.

A few minutes later I realized I had almost no sensation of height, even though we were climbing through 5,000 feet and only a moderate sensation of speed as we moved smoothly over the Texas farmland at more than 200 knots. We flew south about forty miles and passed over the family farm. I had not told Mom I would be flying that day because I knew she would worry. Captain Toedt then turned us gently back to the north, passed over the East Texas State College campus at Commerce, and asked me if I wanted to fly the aircraft.

I gingerly took hold of the control stick, a massive black object with lots of buttons, mounted on the floor between my knees. I tried to make a couple of gentle turns, but I was mostly interested in keeping the jet straight and level. Captain Toedt then took the controls and landed smoothly at Perrin. He taxied in, dropped me off, and picked up another cadet. As I crossed the ramp to the waiting crew bus, the ground felt shaky, but I had survived my first jet aircraft flight.

In 1964, during my last spring in college, I enrolled in the Flight Indoctrination Program (FIP) to learn to fly light airplanes. Captain Toedt and a cadet who had a private pilot's license taught ground school at East Texas State, where we learned about the theory of flight, basic aircraft instruments, and navigation. Twice a week, each FIP student also drove to a nearby town for flight training (the airport runway at Commerce was in disrepair with a hole about midfield large enough to swallow a light plane).

Flight training was taught by a short, stocky civilian I'll call "Mr. Miller." Mr. Miller's flight shack was a one-room, wooden-framed building with a desk, a stove, and a couple of chairs. The walls of the flight shack were covered with shirttails cut from the shirts of previous students who had successfully soloed an aircraft. On each shirttail were written the student's name and the date of this major milestone in a pilot's career. I was awed by the sight and secretly questioned if I would ever be able to do such a thing.

Mr. Miller had a red and silver Cessna 172 powered by a 145 HP Continental engine. On February 6, 1964, he led me through a walk-around preflight inspection of the Cessna. We checked the fuel sumps under the wings for condensed water; checked the wing surfaces for popped rivets; shook the ailerons, elevator, and rudder; kicked the tires; and crawled into the airplane. After briefly explaining the instrument panel and starting procedures, Mr. Miller suddenly said in a loud voice, "Clear the prop!"

He immediately engaged the starter, and the propeller jerked into life. The engine coughed a couple of times and died. He tried it again, and the engine coughed again, caught, and smoothed out. He taxied out to the runway, ran up the engine, checked the magnetos, announced over the radio we were taking off to the south, and rolled onto the runway. He pushed the throttle knob forward slowly, and we picked up speed. We were about halfway down the runway, and Mr. Miller was still adding power. As the end of the runway approached, he pulled back on the steering yoke, and we were airborne, clearing the low trees on the field boundary by about fifty feet. My logbook for that day says we flew two hours of "dual introduction."

Over the next month, I flew a total of twelve hours and soloed on March 3, 1964. The solo flight went fine, but I found myself undulating up and down on final approach as I chased my airspeed. After I landed and was congratulated by Mr. Miller, he cut the tail off of my red shirt and added it to his collection on the wall of the flight shack. I had worn a red shirt that day so my shirttail would stand out from the rest (which were mostly white).

FIP went by rapidly, and most of it was quite interesting. As we flew over the green pastures and farm fields of northeast Texas, we could see redbud trees and wild plums blooming in the creek bottoms. We practiced landings, navigation, emergency procedures, and stalls.

Emergency procedures consisted of Mr. Miller pulling back the throttle to simulate engine failure, and I was supposed to find and line up on a green oat field (which could be counted on to offer a reasonably smooth emergency landing surface). Once we had descended to the point it looked as if I could safely land in the oat field, Mr. Miller would add power, and we would go back up to 2,000 or 3,000 feet and practice some stalls.

Power-off stalls were uncomfortable and somewhat disturbing. I didn't care for the sensation of zero G's as the airplane dropped out from under me. The first power-on stall was terrifying! I thought we were crashing! To do a power-on stall, Mr. Miller left the power set for level flight and pulled the nose of the airplane up into a steep climbing turn to the left. As the airplane ran out of airspeed, the stall warning began to scream, the airplane shuddered, and as the plane stalled, he stomped on the right rudder pedal. The airplane swapped ends and headed straight down, nose first! Dirt, mixed with Mr. Miller's cigarette ashes from the floor, flew up in my face, and I was hurled toward the Plexiglas windscreen. The airplane didn't have a shoulder harness, and my lap belt wasn't nearly tight enough. I thought I was falling through the windscreen! After the aircraft descended 500 feet or so straight down, it gathered enough airspeed to fly again. Mr. Miller pulled back on the yoke, and the aircraft pulled out of the dive and returned to level flight.

I never trusted Mr. Miller after that. He could have warned me about what was going to happen or at least told me to tighten my lap belt. From that day on, however, I have always worn a tight seat belt, in a plane or a car.

After thirty hours of instruction, a Federal Aviation Administration (FAA) check pilot flew over from Dallas to give us our final FIP check rides. Everything was going okay on my check ride until I started my takeoff roll, slowly adding power to "save the engine" as Mr. Miller had taught me. The FAA pilot was horrified. He slammed the throttle to the firewall, and we cleared the trees by several hundred feet. Later at cruise altitude, when the FAA pilot pulled back the throttle and announced "engine failure," I did as I had been taught. I picked out a large green oat field and headed for it. The FAA pilot said, "What about your procedures?" I confessed I had no idea what he was talking about. In the meantime, we had been losing altitude rapidly, and I realized a tall, steel-girdered, electrical pow-erline was blocking my approach to the big oat field!

Just as I realized I couldn't clear the powerline, I happened to notice a narrow oat field running along my side of the pow-erline. So I lined up on that field like I was heading there all along. As we climbed back to altitude, the FAA pilot told me "procedures" included checking the ignition switch, fuel tank selector, and carburetor icing. *I never forgot that lesson.*

After the FAA inspector checked several other FIP students that day and discovered we all performed the same way on take-off and during engine failure emergencies, he passed us but gave Mr. Miller some additional instruction.

In January 1965 I graduated from East Texas State (which had just become a university) with a B.S. degree in general sci-ence and was commissioned a second lieutenant in the United States Air Force. After the graduation and commissioning cere-monies were over, my Paw Paw Ridley pinned my new gold bars on my Class A blue uniform. My fiancée Barbara and I married two weeks later on February 5, 1965, and I got my orders to report to Air Force pilot training.

CHAPTER 3

Air Force Pilot Training

"Flying is a piece of cake as long as you maintain your airspeed, altitude, and sense of humor."

Capt. James Redden, Flight Commander, 1965

I knew Air Force pilot training was going to be serious when the flight surgeons took our footprints and recorded them in our medical records. They said a smoldering pair of flight boots was often all that was left for identification purposes after a bad accident. Another comforting thought!

I reported to pilot training at Webb Air Force Base at Big Spring, Texas, April 21, 1965. I was a twenty-one-year-old second lieutenant. Barbara and I had married in February, and we had everything we owned (except a cow named "Droopy") in a 1958 black Volvo sedan which had been rescued from a junkyard. We had $20 cash left in the world.

2nd Lt. J.L. Green, a friend of mine from Quinlan, Texas, who was just finishing pilot training at Webb as I was starting, said Air Force pilot training was like a four-year college education crammed into one year. J.L. said student pilots would fly for half a day, take an hour of physical training, and participate in academic training the remainder of the day. The training day started at sunrise and ended at sunset, except when there were night flights. There would be no leaves, except at Christmas, and marching and inspections would be scheduled on some Saturdays. As it turned out, J.L. was right; pilot training was extremely tough. It was, however, a tremendous learning experience. Nothing in my life has ever been really difficult since pilot training.

On the first day of pilot training, student pilots were welcomed to Webb AFB and Class 66-G and were told the United States Air Force was about to spend more than $700,000 per student to provide us with the best pilot training in the world. The briefer also said we would be the best crosswind pilots in the world because that was the only kind of winds they had at Webb. He went on to say there would be little difference between the top and the bottom pilot in the graduating class. There was no established washout rate, he said, but not all of us would complete the course and receive our wings. Only those with determination would make it. The briefer then related a story about a British sailor who became deathly ill from seasickness every time he went to sea. The sailor, however, did his best to do his duty even though he suffered from motion sickness all of his life. The briefer said the name of that sailor was Lord Admiral Nelson. The implication, of course, was regardless of any tendency we might have toward motion sickness, we were all expected to do our duty at least as well as the Hero of Trafalgar.

Later that day we were issued flight suits, flight jackets, flight boots, an orange-handled switchblade survival knife, a twenty-four-hour wristwatch, and dog tags. The metal tags provided identification and were worn on a small, beaded chain around the neck. Dog tags were designed to withstand combat (or a bad crash). The information on them included the student's name, Air Force service number, blood type (in case you survived the accident), and religious preference (for last rites, in case you didn't). After being issued our tags and other equipment, we went down to the flight shack and met our new instructor pilots (IPs).

Capt. James Redden, a mean-looking fighter pilot and ex-boxing champ whose call sign was "The Pagan," was the flight commander. 1st Lt. Ron Castleton, a big, stern-looking man whom Captain Redden described as the "world's oldest-looking lieutenant," was my IP. Lieutenant Castleton was a good instructor; he told me what to do, and I did it.

The T-37

We were going to spend the first six months of Air Force pilot training learning to fly the Cessna T-37 "Tweety Bird," a low-winged jet trainer with side-by-side seating and two incredibly loud, screeching engines. Due to the noise of the engines of this "2,000-pound dog whistle," everyone had to wear both rubber ear plugs and headset ear protectors just to walk out on the flight line when T-37s were operating. We were fitted with parachutes, helmets, and oxygen masks; given training in ejection seats and emergency procedures; and started academic training in aircraft engineering and aviation physiology.

Ejection seat training included strapping each student into a special ejection seat on the ground. When the student pulled the ejection seat handles, he was shot up a set of tracks more than twenty-five feet in the air by an explosive charge under the seat. The trip up the tracks was almost instantaneous. I believe I momentarily blacked out from the force of the charge. The first thing I remembered after pulling the handles was clicking slowly back down the tracks toward the ground. The ejection seat technicians sometimes took high-speed photographs of students' faces at the same instant the handles were pulled. Even though the photographs were clear, the students' faces were not recognizable due to the distortion of their facial features. Cheeks were pulled down away from the eyes, and the lips were down where the chin should be, like a sad theater mask. However, we were counting on those ejection seats to get us out of a disabled aircraft in a real emergency.

As part of aviation physiology, we learned what lack of oxygen, or hypoxia, does to the brain. This training included a ride in an altitude chamber, which was actually a heavy steel tank that students and special instructors entered and sat on benches along the wall. The door was shut with an ominous finality, oxygen masks were secured, and air was pumped out to simulate the amount of oxygen found at various altitudes. Students were then told to remove their masks and work simple math problems or puzzles. Under low oxygen conditions, the brain's ability to function rapidly decreases. Various students got sleepy, cold, euphoric, or angry. The purpose of the training was to help the students recognize their own responses to hypoxia so they would realize what was happening if they had a problem with their oxygen equipment. I got cold and sleepy and my fingernails turned blue when I was hypoxic.

Actual flying in the T-37 consisted of four phases: contact, instruments, navigation, and formation. During contact flying, we had visual contact with the ground. During instruments, the student had a hood over the top of his helmet which restricted his vision to the instrument panel and simulated flying in weather. During navigation we practiced getting from point A to point B, and during formation we flew our aircraft in close proximity with other aircraft, following a leader.

For contact flying, Lieutenant Castleton briefed me in the flight shack on what was expected. We checked the scheduling board, and he told me to write our assigned aircraft tail number and training area on the palm of my hand with a ballpoint pen so I wouldn't forget it. We then went next door and got our big white helmets and parachutes and walked out to the flight line.

When I close my eyes today, I can still hear the high-pitched whine of those jet engines, smell the JP-4 jet fuel, and feel the hot jet exhaust blowing across that concrete ramp. Row upon row of metallic-silver T-37s with red-orange safety markings squatted on the ramp in the dazzling sunlight.

We picked out the one with our assigned tail number and did a preflight walk-around inspection much like I had done in light planes. We then stepped into the cockpit. I was in the left seat, and the IP was in the right. The T-37 was built so close to the ground there was just a single foothold built into the side of the aircraft for assistance in getting into the cockpit.

The cockpit checklist was much more complicated than I had seen in light planes. It included fastening parachute harness, securing helmets and oxygen masks, and removing the ejection seat pins. We displayed these pins, with their long red warning ribbons, to the crew chief, and stowed them in a side pocket of the aircraft to be reinstalled upon landing.

When we completed the checklist, Lieutenant Castleton held up two fingers of his gloved hand to indicate to the crew chief he was ready to start Number 2 engine (the one on the right side). He then made a circling windup motion with his index finger. Upon receiving a nod from the crew chief, he engaged the starter and ignition switches, and moved the throttle to the "start" position. Once the right engine was running at idle, he repeated the sequence for the left engine.

Lieutenant Castleton requested and received radio clearance to taxi from Ground Control. He then held up both fists in front of his face with thumbs extended outward as a signal for the crew chief to pull the wheel chocks. Once the chocks were removed, the crew chief used hand signals to direct us out of the parking area. The crew chief then did something that is not required on the flight line but I have seen many times since. He came to attention and threw us a crisp military salute!

The lieutenant taxied the aircraft out to the runway, received takeoff clearance from "Horntoad" (call sign of the Webb Control Tower), and shoved the throttles forward to 100 percent power. The T-37 was much noisier and faster than a light plane, but the acceleration still was not what I expected of a jet aircraft. Once we were safely airborne, Lieutenant Castleton let me take the controls, and we headed out to one of the assigned training areas north of Big Spring, where he showed me some of the basic flight characteristics of the T-37. As I recall, the Air Force was very serious about everyone staying in their assigned area to avoid accidents. Besides the horizontal boundaries, we were not supposed to get below 12,000 feet or above 23,000 feet.

After we had burned off some fuel and were at a lighter weight, we headed over to an auxiliary Air Force landing field known as "Woodpecker," which was located just north of Colorado City. After demonstrating an overhead traffic pattern and landing, Lieutenant Castleton let me try one. I was all over the sky. It was even harder than it looked. To do an overhead pattern, you descended to 1,000 above the runway, checked carefully for other aircraft, stated your call sign over the radio and "Initial" (indicating you were at the initial approach point of the traffic pattern). You then flew directly down the runway at an airspeed of 200 knots and 1,000 feet above the ground headed in the same direction you planned to land (this gave you a quick look at the field and a final check of the windsock). As the far end of the runway disappeared under the nose of your aircraft, you dropped the speed brakes, made an abrupt 60-degree bank left turn, and pulled back on the control stick hard enough to keep the aircraft from losing altitude. In a T-37, this was a "2 G" turn, or twice the force of gravity. At this point, the aircraft, and your body, weighed twice what they did just a moment ago. The first few times you did this, it was disorienting and uncomfortable, but you had to maintain the same pull until you had completed a 180-degree turn and were headed back the direction you had come from. Now you were on the "downwind" part of the pattern, flying parallel to the runway and about a half mile to the east. You lowered your landing gear and held this heading and altitude, all the time watching out for other aircraft, until the approach end of the runway was even with your left wing tip. At that point, you announced your call sign and "Final turn" over the radio. You lowered your flaps and began making a left turn back toward the runway, but this time you didn't hold the control stick back as tightly. You wanted the aircraft to descend smoothly during the final turn so you would complete the turn on a short final approach at just the right height and with exactly 100 knots of airspeed. Although it took a full minute to complete the final turn, it seemed like about five seconds.

After several more contact flights in the training area and at Woodpecker, we made a full stop at Woodpecker, and Lieutenant Castleton got out and told me to make a couple of solo landings. I did fine on the first traffic pattern and landing, but on the second pattern, as I made my 60-degree bank turn from initial approach to downwind, I pulled too hard and climbed several hundred feet in less time than it takes to tell it. I then had to descend to get back to the correct altitude on downwind so I could turn final. In pilot talk, I was now mentally behind the aircraft, meaning I was worrying about things I had done wrong and not about what I should be doing. I remembered to put the landing gear handle down, but I didn't get it all the way down into the locked position, and the landing gear did not come down. The landing gear warning horn was blowing so loudly, I couldn't think! Fortunately, Lieutenant Castleton was in the mobile control tower at Woodpecker, and when he saw I didn't have the gear down, he told me over the radio to "Go around!" I managed to land safely the next time around. When the lieutenant got back in the aircraft, all he said was, "You got a little high in the turn, didn't you?" He didn't even mention the landing gear. He didn't have to! I never made that mistake again.

My landings slowly improved, and I got better at reading

the wind, judging my touchdown point, compensating for "ground effect," and feeling for the runway. One evening after I had just made the final landing of the day, Lieutenant Castleton gave me his supreme compliment when he said in his gravelly voice, "I'll say one thing for you, George, you can land this airplane."

About this same time, we began learning the basics of aerobatics. Air Force IPs were not like my civilian instructor, Mr. Miller. Air Force IPs carefully cleaned up the cockpit area, stowed any loose equipment, explained what they were going to do, and then talked you through it. The first aerobatic maneuver we were shown was a split S. I was not with Lieutenant Castleton that day, but the substitute IP went through the usual routine, visually cleared the area below the aircraft, pulled the nose of the aircraft up in a steep climb, extended the speed breaks, and smoothly rolled the aircraft over on its back. From inside the cockpit, it looked like the world had just turned upside down! Then the IP pulled back hard on the stick, and we completed the bottom half of a loop. That was apparently more than my body could take. When we were straight and level again, I threw up and completely filled my cheeks to the bursting point with sour-tasting vomit. However, I remembered Captain Redden's orders on this subject and slowly swallowed it all back down. The IP realized what had happened and wisely decided I had had enough flight instruction for the day.

Over the next several weeks, we were introduced to other aerobatic maneuvers. We flew loops, aileron rolls, barrel rolls, Immelmans, lazy 8's, chandelles, cloverleaves, and others all in an unpressurized, Plexiglas-covered cockpit during the middle of a West Texas summer. During these maneuvers, we would often pull 4 G's and sometimes as much as 6 G's, or six times the force of gravity. We had to tighten our stomach and leg muscles during the turns to keep our blood from pooling in our lower extremities and causing blackouts as the blood left our brains. We would come back from contact flights exhausted, our flight suits soaked with sweat. I managed to keep my motion sickness pretty well under control whenever I was flying the aircraft, but when an IP was demonstrating a new maneuver, I would really get queasy because I couldn't anticipate which direction the aircraft was going to move. After one aerobatic flight, we had finished the hard stuff, and Lieutenant Castleton had made the final landing. We were taxiing down the runway, and I had just looked down and leaned over to the left in the cockpit to retrieve the ejection seat pins when the lieutenant turned the aircraft on to the taxiway. That unexpected motion with my head down was more than I could take. I threw up again, but this time there was no holding it. We were not permitted to carry "barf bags," since this was thought to encourage airsickness, but I managed to completely fill a leather flight glove without losing a drop. That was the last time I really got sick in an airplane, but for the rest of my flying career I continued to be uncomfortable when another pilot was flying the aircraft.

Three of my fellow student pilots never got past these first few weeks of pilot training. One had no depth perception and could not tell how high he was during landings. Another could not get over airsickness, and a third was just scared. They washed out, and we never heard from them again. This was years before Tom Wolfe's book *The Right Stuff* was published so we didn't know what to call it, but only those in our class with the "right stuff" continued to fly.

We needed the right stuff as we flew more and more solo flights out in the training area. Once our IPs were reasonably sure we wouldn't kill ourselves or bend our airplanes, we were sent out to practice aerobatics on our own. On my very first solo contact flight, I got to my assigned area, carefully cleaned up the cockpit, visually checked for traffic, and pulled up into a loop. When I was absolutely vertical, going straight up, I looked over my left shoulder and saw another T-37 in the direction I was planning to complete my loop. The other T-37 was probably safely out of the way over in his own training area, but we had been cautioned so often about avoiding other aircraft I didn't want to complete the loop in his direction. In retrospect, there were a lot of things I could have done, such as rolling the aircraft 90 or 180 degrees and completing the loop in another direction, but I couldn't think what to do. So the aircraft just continued straight up until it ran out of airspeed. At that point, it could have gone into a hammerhead stall or a tailspin or some other terrible maneuver, but the T-37 is a forgiving aircraft. I simply pushed the stick gently forward out of the top of the vertical climb, and it flew off straight and level as if nothing had happened. I told some of my fellow students what I had done, but I never did tell Lieutenant Castleton.

Another "near miss" occurred a few days later, when I was returning to base after a solo contact flight. Our IPs had frequently reminded us that two jets meeting head-on at 250 knots have a combined closure rate of 500 knots, and this can happen in the blink of an eye. I was, therefore, particularly alert as I departed my training area and began descending through 18,000 feet. All of a sudden, I saw a black dot directly in front of me closing at a fantastic rate! I jerked the stick violently to the right to avoid the collision. When I had my aircraft under control again, I glanced over my shoulder in the direction I expected to see the other aircraft, but there was nothing there but blue sky! Mystified, I visually cleared in all directions and continued my flight home.

Suddenly, there he was again, straight in front of me! Again I took evasive action, but this time, I kept my eye on the other aircraft. All of a sudden, I realized the other "aircraft" was actually a common house fly flying around in the cockpit with me. No wonder he was able to appear and disappear so quickly. Although he had given me a pretty good scare, I had to admire his ability to fly around in an unpressurized cockpit at 18,000 feet.

The next thing we learned was spins. Tailspins have been dreaded by pilots since the first airplanes, and a number of pilots were killed by tailspins until someone figured out a way to recover from this situation. In a tailspin, an aircraft doesn't respond to the control stick like you think it should. Regardless of how hard you pull back on the control stick, the aircraft will not come out of its terrifying, spinning, nose-down dive toward the earth.

To intentionally spin a T-37, you set the throttles at idle, pull the stick back into a climb, and continue to pull the stick back as the aircraft runs out of airspeed. When the aircraft stalls and starts to fall out from under you, you continue to hold the stick all the way back in your lap while you stomp on one of the rudder pedals. Suddenly, the aircraft flips over and points almost straight down. The whole world is spinning around and shaking before your eyes. This is not a pleasant sensation!

To recover from a spin, you stomp on the opposite rudder pedal. The aircraft stops spinning, but it is still pointed straight down. At this point, you pop the stick all the way *forward* and then release it. If everything goes well, the aircraft can then be pulled gently out of the dive and returned to normal flight.

One of our IPs told us that when he was a student, his IP took him up to demonstrate spins. On the very first spin, the IP got the aircraft into a spin but couldn't get out of it. The aircraft was spinning and shaking, the altimeter was unwinding, and the student saw his instructor struggling with the controls. At that point the student, who had never seen a spin before, had the courage to ask, "Sir, is something wrong?" The IP did not respond but continued to struggle with the controls. The student asked again and shook the IP with no response. The student then pushed himself back in his seat and pulled the ejection seat handles. His parachute opened safely, and he landed unhurt, but his IP rode the plane into the ground and was killed. Another hard lesson learned.

To me, instrument flying was even tougher than contact flying. It was a very unnatural feeling to trust the little dials and gauges on the instrument panel when they were telling you something entirely different from what your body was telling you. When you had the hood on, or when you were in actual weather, you might feel as if you were straight and level but actually you could be in a descending right turn or any other maneuver. On my first radar approach, when the radar controller on the ground was telling me by radio which headings to fly and which altitudes to maintain, I was concentrating so hard on flying instruments I could not hear the commands from the controller. My mind simply tuned him out. I had all I could handle, just keeping the aircraft straight and level on instruments. I slowly got better, but for my entire flying career, instruments remained the most difficult part of my flying.

Night flying combined some of the elements of both contact and instrument flying, but I really enjoyed night flying. The air was generally very smooth at night, with little wind, and the moon, stars, oilfield flares, city lights, and airfield runway lights were beautiful to see. On my very first night flight, however, I was with another IP, and he said, "Would you like to call your wife?" I had no idea what he was talking about. He explained we could radio the Air Defense Command radar station at Sweetwater and get them to place a phone patch telephone call back to Barbara at Big Spring. Well, we called up Barb, and I had just said hello and told her I was calling from my airplane when the phone patch went dead. We were unable to reestablish contact, and Barb was white as a sheet when I got home two hours later. She thought something terrible had gone wrong with the aircraft and I was calling to say a final goodbye.

Navigation flying was something we looked forward to. It was a chance to go out and see some different country, shoot some instrument approaches at a different military base, and maybe see the nightlife in another city. Navigation flying, however, also offered additional chances to mess up—*big time*. On an out-and-back navigation flight to Amarillo, Texas, I was flying with a substitute IP. He was flying the first leg of the trip, and I was observing. He leveled off at our assigned altitude for an eastbound leg and then turned the aircraft over to me several minutes later. I reached the end of the eastbound leg and turned back to the west. This change of heading required a change of altitude, so I started to climb an additional 1,000 feet. At that moment we both were horrified to realize we were 2,000 feet, not 1,000 feet, below our new westbound altitude. The IP had inadvertently leveled off 1,000 feet too low, and I had not caught it. This was a lesson I remembered for a long time.

On my first overnight navigation flight, I was again paired with a substitute IP. Lieutenant Castleton told me he didn't know this IP, but he guessed he would be all right. Both the substitute IP and I had relatives in the Dallas area, and we planned to end up at Dallas Naval Air Station and spend the night with our relatives. That was not to be. When we got to Base Operations at Webb to file our flight plan, we found out Dallas was socked in with weather. In fact, the only place open within T-37 flying distance of Webb was James Connally Air Force Base at Waco. There were about ten other students and their IPs at Base Ops at the same time we were. We all got the same weather briefing, and we all went to Waco.

By the time we got to Waco, it was dark, and all of the IPs had their students practicing radar approaches at James Connally. Around and around we all went. This was a lot more traffic than the controllers at James Connally were used to, but they were doing their best, and we were getting good practice. We eventually got down to minimum fuel, and the yellow warning light on our instrument panel came on. We were on final approach, so I announced "Minimum fuel" to the IP, indicating I was planning a full stop. He apparently thought I needed additional training because he said, "That only applies back at home base." I was shocked! However, he was the instructor and I was the student, so I went around and entered downwind for another radar approach. Because of all the other traffic in the radar pattern, it was difficult to hear the radar controllers over the radio, so we continued on downwind as we had been assigned. We kept going farther and farther north and eventually we lost sight of the lights at Waco and James Connally. We were getting lower on fuel, and we still hadn't received any instructions from the radar controller to turn back toward Waco.

Finally, the IP got on the radio and asked for instructions. There was an embarrassed pause from the controller. In all of the excitement, the controller had lost us. He thought all of the T-37s had landed! He told us to turn immediately to a heading of 180 degrees. We drove for quite a long time, and eventually we could see the lights at James Connally. By then, the IP knew he had really messed up. He took control of the aircraft and flew, at reduced throttle, back toward the lights. I quietly sat back in my seat and extended my hands down near the ejection seat handles. If the engines coughed, I was leaving!

When we finally got back to the glide slope and the controller said, "Begin descent," it looked as if we might make it. But both fuel gauges now showed "Zero"! We did land safely, however, made a very short landing roll, and turned off and parked on a ramp right beside the main runway. After the fuel truck driver refilled our tanks, he walked up to us and, in a very concerned voice said he had just put eight more gallons of fuel in our aircraft than it was designed to hold! The IP brushed him off like that happened all the time.

"The rest of the story," as news commentator Paul Harvey

would say, happened the next morning when our left engine wouldn't start. When the crew chiefs opened up the cowling, they found an oil line had severed, and the eight-gallon oil reservoir was filled with fuel instead of lubricating oil. That's where the extra eight gallons of fuel went when the aircraft was refueled the night before. It may also explain how the aircraft was able to stay in the air with empty fuel tanks. We were burning the lubricating oil from our left engine as fuel. It was either an incredible coincidence, or the Good Lord was looking out for us that night.

Formation flying was terrifying at first. After all, it had been drilled into us over and over not to get close to another aircraft in flight. Now we were being told to fly right up to another T-37 and maintain position on his wing or tail. When flying on the wing, known as "echelon" or "fingertip formation," we simply lined up on the 40-degree angle made by his wing flap hinge and the red ejection seat warning decal on his fuselage. We then pulled forward and inward along this angle until our cockpit was even with his tail. In this position, the tips of our wings nearly overlapped, and our fuselages were only thirty feet apart. However, with a lot of practice, it became easy to maintain this position regardless of where the leader went as long as he did it smoothly. We even got to where we could take off and land on someone's wing. It is actually much easier to be the wingman than it is to be the leader of a formation flight. *The leader has to think!* The wingman just stays in position.

The first six months of pilot training went by rapidly, and those of us who were still around moved on to T-38s.

The T-38

The most memorable airplane flight I have ever experienced was my first flight in a supersonic Northrop T-38 "Talon." Instead of a short, squat, ugly plane like the T-37, the T-38 was a beautiful, needle-nosed, gleaming-white aircraft which looked like it was going supersonic just sitting on the parking ramp. T-38s cost $1 million apiece in 1960 dollars.

My new IP, Captain Holcomb, was a slightly built, soft-spoken Southerner who looked like he could fly anything. He briefed me on the flight and told me I would be in the front seat and he would be in the back. He said he would make the takeoff and for me to just watch. The T-38 had an extremely sensitive control stick, he warned, and he closed the briefing by saying in a very forceful voice, "Don't you touch anything on takeoff!" I replied, "Yes, sir!"

We went out to the aircraft, did a walk around, and climbed in. This thing was so tall you had to have a ladder to reach the cockpit. We got strapped in, started the engines, and taxied out to the runway. I noticed the instrument panel had even more gauges and dials than the T-37, but the T-38's instrument panel seemed to be better organized.

Captain Holcomb got takeoff clearance from the tower, lined up the T-38 on the centerline of the runway, stopped the aircraft, and then pumped up and locked the brakes with the foot pedals. The T-38 rocked slightly back and forth on its landing gear struts as though it were a sprinter preparing for the starting gun. As he brought the throttles up to 100 percent rpms, the jet blast coming from the twin tailpipes of our General Electric J85-GE-5 turbojet engines created more than 2,600 pounds of thrust. I could feel the aircraft straining against its locked brakes. It felt as though our rubber tires were actually scrubbing down the runway. This awesome power raised the rear of the aircraft like a cat about to spring. I remember thinking, *We're fixin' to go for a ride!*

He checked the engine instruments, released the brakes, and shoved the throttles into "afterburner," pouring raw fuel into the hot exhaust pipes and increasing our engine power to more than 3,800 pounds of thrust. As the aircraft shot down the runway, I was pushed back in my seat, and I could feel the air being squeezed out of the parachute strapped to my back as we accelerated faster and faster. I noticed that the thousand-foot markers along the side of the runway were going by like slats on a picket fence!

Captain Holcomb gently eased back on the stick as we flashed through 155 knots, and the T-38 leaped into the air as we continued to accelerate. He immediately cleaned up the gear and flaps. As I recall, the pilot was supposed to get the gear and flaps up before passing through 240 knots, or the windstream would tear them off. The captain left the engines in afterburner, and I could still feel air being forced from my parachute as we continued to accelerate. We were really moving now, climbing like a homesick angel! The world looked distorted, and the clouds were zipping by. The altimeter needle was winding up like a runaway clock, and the vertical velocity indicator was showing an incredible rate of climb. Only two minutes after we began our takeoff roll, Captain Holcomb leveled off at Flight Level 300 (30,000 feet).

He left the engines in afterburner, and almost instantly the aircraft went supersonic! We slipped smoothly through the once-feared "sound barrier," which Air Force Capt. Chuck Yeager had broken in the Bell X-1 rocket plane "Glamorous Glennis" for the first time only nineteen years before. There was no physical sensation at all. We didn't even hear the sonic boom we created; it was behind us. The only indication in the cockpit we were now supersonic was when the airspeed indicator and other air-pressure instruments jerked momentarily and then settled down as the shockwave passed the end of the pitot tube. We were now traveling faster than the speed of sound, or "Mach 1," more than 600 knots (700 miles per hour). At this point, Captain Holcomb pulled the throttles out of afterburner, and we slowed to subsonic speed.

The captain then demonstrated an aileron roll and let me try one. He said not to push the control stick all the way over to the side because the T-38 could complete three aileron rolls per second at maximum stick deflection. This would send the aircraft spinning through the air like a rifle bullet and could be very disorienting to an inexperienced pilot.

He also talked me through a rudder roll. He said, "Gently, press down on the left rudder pedal and hold it." As I did, the nose of the aircraft pulled up and to the left, and we rolled over on our back and completed sort of a tight, nose-outward barrel roll. He said, "As you can see, the rudder on the T-38 can get you into trouble. Don't ever use the rudder pedals in this aircraft again! You can get all the control you need with just the control stick."

He then took control of the aircraft, descended from altitude, zipped around the traffic pattern at 195 knots, slowed to 175 knots on final approach, and landed. As we were walking back to the Flight Shack, he said to me, "Do you think you will be able to solo this aircraft with another ten hours of flight time?" It did not seem remotely possible at the time, but ten hours later I was sent out solo.

Flying the T-38 was like holding a tiger by the tail. I always felt as though I were aiming it rather than flying it. Things happened so much faster in a T-38 than they did in any other aircraft I had ever flown. On top of everything else, you had to keep recalculating your traffic pattern and final approach speeds as you burned off fuel and the aircraft became lighter in weight. The T-38 came down final approach nose high and riding on its powerful exhaust. It was a beautiful aircraft to watch and a fantastic aircraft to fly, but it was very sobering to be sent out to make your first solo flight in that sleek, white jet.

Because of the nose-high landing attitude of the T-38, I still had some trouble judging whether I was making a proper landing approach. So on my first solo, I went around without touching down on two of my five landing attempts. I got much better with practice, but I never took a T-38 landing for granted. Even after it was back on the ground, and the tires had chirped and smoked, you had to hold the nose up for aerodynamic braking until the aircraft had slowed down to the point where you no longer felt like you were riding a rocket.

On one occasion, Barbara and the wives of other student pilots were permitted on to go out to the mobile control hut at the end of the T-38 runway to watch our landings. Although our voices sounded unnatural and garbled over the radio, each wife, with a little assistance, was able to identify her husband by his call sign when he called initial and final approach. Knowing the wives were there, I wanted to make a good impression. Barbara got to see one of my best ever landings (very smooth with almost no tire smoke). I was concentrating so hard on the approach and landing I never even stole a glance at my admiring audience.

Besides the ever-present crosswinds at Webb, there were numerous whirlwinds or "dust devils" during the summer months. One time, when I was up in the control tower at Webb, I recall counting twenty whirlwinds, some towering 1,000 feet or more in the air, moving slowly across the West Texas plains. When you could see them, you could avoid them, but whirlwinds had a tendency to lose their dust loads when they crossed the grassy area around the runways. One of our IPs was making a landing one day, and he hit a whirlwind he couldn't see just as he was touching down. The whirlwind instantly rolled his aircraft up in a 90-degree bank, but he was able to go to afterburner and fly the thing sideways out of danger. A truly remarkable feat!

Instrument flying in a T-38 was even more unbelievable than it had been in the T-37. In a T-38, the IP was in the front seat and the student in the back seat under a canvas hood, which completely covered the inside of the rear cockpit. The IP lined the aircraft up on the centerline of the runway, and said, "You've got it." The student then was expected to make a blind takeoff, fly a standard instrument departure, navigate across country to another Air Force base, enter a holding pattern at 20,000 feet, receive clearance from air traffic control, make an instrument approach to the landing field, go "missed approach" at 200 feet above the runway, fly back home, and make another instrument approach down to "minimums." Then if the student was still alive, the IP would take control of the aircraft and complete the landing. For me, this kind of flying was mentally exhausting since you were always under the hood and there was never a moment to relax during the entire hour-and-fifteen-minute flight. It was, however, excellent training for future flying in actual weather.

For aerobatic flying in the T-38, we were issued an additional piece of equipment we didn't have in the T-37. This was a "G-suit." A G-suit was a pair of trousers with inflatable balloons in the legs and around the waist. The G-suit had a rubber hose that you connected to the aircraft during preflight. When you started pulling G's during aerobatics, a sensor in the aircraft automatically inflated the balloons, tightened the G-suit around the lower part of your body, and prevented your blood from rushing to your lower extremities. This permitted the pilot to more comfortably fly high G maneuvers without blacking out from lack of blood (and oxygen) in the brain. We called these G-suits our "Go fast pants."

Much of our aerobatic flying in the T-38 was in formation. It was really challenging, but it also gave us a tremendous feeling of accomplishment to be able to do what we were doing. Once we got used to it, flying on someone's wing or on their tail was a piece of cake. The only time I ever had a sensation of height in an aircraft was when I was in trail formation behind another T-38 and we were coming down the back side of a loop, headed straight toward the ground. In this position, the twin tailpipes of the T-38 only fifty feet ahead of me looked just like the top of a tall chimney I was falling into. Other than that, T-38 formation flying on someone's wing or tail was almost effortless. Sometimes I even had trouble concentrating on what I was doing. I recall flying solo on my instructor's wing one time, and we were flying over-the-top aerobatics. The sun, earth, and sky were rolling around me in constant motion, and we were upside down, but I caught myself daydreaming about what I would be doing when I got off work that evening. This can be dangerous in an aircraft flying at better than 500 knots.

T-38 navigation flights were also fast and exciting. An automobile trip from Big Spring to Dallas, which took nearly six hours of hard driving on Interstate 20, could easily be made in thirty minutes in a T-38 without even using the afterburner.

We also flew one low-level navigation flight in the T-38. The low-level flight was flown at 250 knots and only 500 feet above the ground to simulate a fighter-bomber's approach to a target below enemy radar. The world looks entirely different at that altitude and airspeed. The flight plan had various checkpoints, such as bridges or other easily recognized objects which were in view for only a few seconds before you took a new heading to the next checkpoint. If you failed to find your next checkpoint on an actual combat mission, you would be forced to climb enough to regain your bearings, but this would expose you to enemy radar. Our flight, however, went great, and we successfully "bombed" the circular automobile test track near San Angelo on time, exactly to the second.

I recall two night navigation flights in T-38s which were exciting. On the first, I was returning from Amarillo to Webb solo on a nice clear night when suddenly there was a brilliant red light flashing all around my aircraft, the way it looks when a police car pulls up behind a speeder. I thought I had just had a near miss with another aircraft! After a moment or two, however, I realized I had flown into a thin, nearly invisible cloud which was reflecting my own red-flashing, anti-collision beacons back into my cockpit.

On the other occasion, I had an IP in the back, and I was flying south toward Abilene, Texas, at Flight Level 260 (26,000 feet). It was a beautiful night with a full moon, and the ground was lighted by dozens of oil well flares. You could see forever. I was flying along, fat, dumb, and happy, when I realized I couldn't see Abilene, my next checkpoint. At that altitude and with that much visibility, I should have been able to see the lights of Abilene from more than 100 miles away, but there was nothing but blackness on the ground ahead of me. I rechecked my map and navigational instruments. The Morse Code identifier I was listening to through my headset indicated I had set in the proper frequency for "ABI," my TACAN needle showed Abilene was directly on the nose of my aircraft, and the DME (distance measuring equipment) showed Abilene was only twenty-five miles away. However, when I looked outside, there was no indication Abilene had ever existed at that spot! I frantically rechecked all the instruments again. They still appeared okay, but the DME now showed twelve miles, and there was still no sign of Abilene.

I was just at the point where I was going to admit to the IP something was terribly wrong and I was lost, when Abilene popped into view. It had been completely hidden from view behind a small cloud! Normally, under those conditions, a cloud would have shown up very white and recognizable in the moonlight. That particular cloud, however, was misshapen just enough for part of the cloud to cast a shadow on the rest of the cloud, so the whole cloud—and the city of Abilene—completely disappeared. I never did tell the IP I had misplaced Abilene, but I did relearn a valuable lesson. *Trust your instruments.*

After a long, exhausting, and exhilarating year, pilot training came to an end. I was both glad it was over and sorry to see it end. It was the biggest adventure I had ever had. There was a tremendous camaraderie in pilot training, and many of my classmates became lifelong friends. Looking back, I sometimes find it hard to believe all we went through. For a schoolboy who couldn't fly a paper airplane and was scared of heights, I had done pretty well in Air Force pilot training. I graduated right in the middle of my class in both academics and flight proficiency.

We received our silver Air Force wings in a Saturday morning ceremony on the Webb AFB Flight Line on May 10, 1966. A flight of four gleaming-white T-38s streaked over the reviewing stand near the end of the ceremony, followed by an exhibition by the U.S. Air Force aerobatic team, "The Thunderbirds." Mom, my brother Mike, and Barbara's mom and dad came out to Webb to see me graduate. After the ceremony, Barbara pinned my wings on my uniform shirt. It was a very proud moment for me. I recall thinking, however, *If pilot training is this tough, how difficult is it going to be when we get to an operational Air Force squadron?*

We were assigned to our next squadron based on our class standing and our choice of aircraft and major air command. As I recall, there were about thirty different combinations of aircraft types and major air commands to choose from. The list had F-4 fighters, RF-4 reconnaissance aircraft, and C-130 cargo planes to the Tactical Air Command, Pacific Air Command, and European Air Command. There were F-101 and F-102 fighter-interceptors to the Air Defense Command, T-37s and T-38s to the Air Training Command, and B-52 bombers and KC-135 tankers to the Strategic Air Command. The top student out of all six Air Force pilot training bases, nationwide, who graduated on the same day we did got his first choice. The next highest-ranking student got his choice if it wasn't already taken, and so on down the list.

Vietnam was heating up, I had a wife and a baby on the way, and I was not particularly anxious for an overseas fighter assignment. I got my fifth choice, a KC-135 jet tanker.

CHAPTER 4

JET TANKER TRAINING

"Breakaway! Breakaway! Breakaway!"
Boom operator's call for an emergency
separation during air refueling

When we married, I told Barbara that as an Air Force officer's wife, she should be ready to go anywhere in the world on a moment's notice. She said she was ready. However, as it turned out, the only place outside of Texas she got to go with me in the Air Force was to jet tanker training at Castle Air Force Base in the San Joaquin Valley of California.

We traveled from Texas to California by way of Pullman, Washington, to visit my brother Larry, who was going to graduate school at Washington State University. At the time, I was still suffering from "jet pilot syndrome" (Barbara will tell you I never got over it). I had "the need for speed," and I was really uncomfortable moving slow. As I recall, we made the trip from Dallas, Texas, to Pullman (a distance of 2,000 miles) in our 1964 Chevrolet Malibu, and only five cars overtook and passed us in that whole distance. No one passed us on the plains from Dallas to Denver, but I believe the drivers of those five cars who passed us in the mountains west of Denver must have been crazy! In retrospect, driving like that was not very smart, but I had a jet pilot's reflexes at the time. We made it fine.

We had a nice visit with Larry and his wife, Janice, and then wandered southwest through the coastal redwood forests, took

Highway 1 along the Pacific Coast, passed along the north side of San Francisco Bay, and crossed the Coastal Mountain Range into the Central Valley of California. Along with our trip out through the Rocky Mountains and Yellowstone National Park, we had had a very pleasant vacation leave.

Jet tanker training was considerably more relaxed than jet pilot training had been. We had academic training in the classroom, instrument training in Link flight simulators, and mission planning and actual training flights in the KC-135 jet tanker a couple of times a week. Unlike pilot training, where the only students were student pilots, in tanker school, my student flight crew included another young pilot and myself who were being trained as copilots, a student navigator, and a student boom operator. We also had an instructor pilot, an instructor navigator, and an instructor boom operator who flew with us on every training mission.

The Boeing KC-135 "Stratotanker" was certainly different from the T-38. For one thing, it did not have ejection seats. In an emergency, you were supposed to hang on to a little steel bar and then drop through a hole in the floor, but for most of my Air Force career no one had ever successfully bailed out of a KC-135.

The 135 was also a huge aircraft, a real "aluminum overcast." It was 130 feet wide, 41 feet tall, and weighed over 100,000 pounds *empty*. It could carry nearly 200,000 pounds (100 tons) of JP-4 jet fuel which could be either offloaded to a receiver or burned by the tanker. Its four Pratt and Whitney, water-injection, dual axial flow, J57-P-59W turbojet engines delivered a combined thrust of 52,000 pounds. Fully loaded, it accelerated slowly on takeoff and used most of a three-mile-long runway. The KC-135 was a ground-loving hog, but in the air it was known as "The Cadillac of the Air Force" for its comfort and smooth ride. Its engines, airframe, and fuel system were similar to the Boeing 707 jet airliner. The KC-135 had an air refueling flying boom which could be flown around in circles and telescoped in and out by the boom operator, who laid on his stomach and looked out a window in the back of the aircraft.

The pilot and copilot operated all the systems and flew the aircraft, the navigator got you to the place where you were supposed to meet your receiver aircraft, and the boom operator made the hookup with the receiver. A boom operator position was considered a plush assignment for an enlisted man. Boom operators, who were usually senior sergeants, often joked they were the only enlisted men in the Air Force who had three officers just to take them to work.

A typical refueling mission started with extensive mission planning on the day before the actual flight. Mission planning included computation of takeoff and climb data; preparation of fuel logs and copilot and navigator's maps; and a review of expected weather and takeoff, refueling, and landing times. It also included a recheck of call signs, receiver type, refueling track location, altitudes, airspeeds, tanker fuel loads, receiver off loads, emergency procedures, and many other items. It was a standing joke you were ready to fly a KC-135 only when the weight of the paperwork equaled the weight of the aircraft.

The actual tanker mission typically started with a precise, on-time takeoff, a standard instrument departure, a climb to Flight Level 280 (28,000 feet), and an entry into a 20-mile long, racetrack-shaped, holding pattern at an exact, prearranged spot in the sky where you waited for your receiver. The tanker and the receiver made radio and radar contact when they were more than 100 miles apart, and the tanker turned toward the receiver when they were 70 miles apart. On a really clear day, I could see a B-52 bomber 28 miles away. At 22 miles, the tanker pilot began a 30-degree bank, 180-degree turn to the left directly into the path of the receiver. By the time the tanker's turn was completed, the receiver should be directly behind the tanker and 1,000 feet below. The receiver then climbed up to the tanker's altitude and flew trail formation behind the tanker.

As a large receiver aircraft, like a B-52, moved into refueling position, it pushed a bow wave of air ahead of it which caused the tanker's tail to rise and required the tanker pilot to trim off the excess elevator pressure. Once the receiver was in proper position, the boom operator flew the boom around as needed and made the hookup. The boom operator then said "Contact" over the radio, a yellow refueling light came on the tanker's instrument panel, and the tanker copilot turned on four powerful air refueling pumps which could offload more than 6,500 pounds of fuel per minute. Even at this rate, it often took nearly thirty minutes to completely refuel a B-52. The optimum B-52 refueling speed of 255 knots was increased to as much as 320 knots for fighter aircraft like the F-105.

If the receiver aircraft got too close during refueling or some other emergency occurred, the boom operator would shout the tanker's call sign over the radio and the words, "Breakaway! Breakaway! Breakaway!" When he heard a breakaway call, the receiver pilot chopped his throttles to idle and descended 1,000 feet, while the tanker pilot shoved his throttles forward to full military power, waited until he heard his boom operator say, "Clear to climb," and then climbed 1,000 feet to ensure safe separation. We practiced breakaway procedures on training missions, but actual emergency breakaways were rare. When you heard an unanticipated breakaway call, however, it sure got your attention!

Once the refueling was completed, the aircraft would separate, and each aircraft continued with its assigned mission. For the tanker, this usually meant a climb to Flight Level 400 (40,000 feet) or above and a practice navigation leg for the navigator. Navigation legs were a time for the pilots to relax, eat their flight lunch, and watch the scenery go by. We could often see the Pacific Ocean to the west, Mount Shasta to the north, the Sierra Nevadas to the east, and San Francisco Bay to the south. Lake Tahoe and Crater Lake also showed up beautifully from the air and on radar. After the navigation leg was completed, it was time for the pilots to practice instrument approaches and landings. As usual, I continued to struggle with instrument flying, but landings soon became a piece of cake even in that huge airplane with the cockpit high in the air.

The three months of tanker training went by rapidly, and Barbara and I enjoyed our time in California very much. Bill Causey, my friend and classmate from Pilot Training Class 66-G at Webb, was going through B-52 training at Castle at the same time I was going through KC-135 training, and our families saw each other often. Bill and Joan and their daughter, Stacy, went to San Francisco with us once to see the sights. Barb and Joan picked peaches in the local orchards, and I threw my boomerang at the jackrabbits in the field across from our house on Applegate Road. Barb and I also visited Yosemite and Sequoia

National Parks. We never saw a cloud in the sky during our entire summer in the Central Valley of California—absolutely clear blue skies overhead. On really clear days, we could even see the Sierra Nevadas to the east and the Coastal Mountain Range to the west from our house.

When I graduated and it came time to go back to Texas, Barb and I thought we would drive nonstop back to Dallas, see the folks, and then report to my new assignment at Abilene, Texas, all in five days. We drove for twenty-four hours straight and got as far as Amarillo, Texas, before we had to stop and get a motel. It was nice to see the familiar big, white, fluffy, cumulus clouds in New Mexico and Texas again. I also recall eating at the Big Texan Steak Ranch in Amarillo, which offered a seventy-two-ounce steak free if you could eat it all. It was good to be back in Texas!

CHAPTER 5

"PEACE IS OUR PROFESSION"

Motto of the Strategic Air Command (SAC)

"Peace is Our Profession" may seem like an unusual motto for an organization whose primary mission was to drop nuclear bombs on the Soviet Union. For nearly four decades, SAC bomber crews and their support tankers trained for this mission, sat "alert" in concrete bunkers beside their armed aircraft, and were prepared to go to war if the Klaxon sounded. My new assignment with the 917th Air Refueling Squadron at Dyess Air Force Base at Abilene, Texas, was part of that mission.

I had heard the SAC motto and seen the SAC emblem (an armored fist holding an olive branch and a bunch of lightning bolts). However, I didn't fully realize how seriously SAC took itself and its mission regarding the "Cold War," "Nuclear Deterrents," and "America's First Strike Capability" until I reported in at Dyess in September 1966.

The Cuban Missile Crisis of 1962, when America was at the brink of nuclear war, was still fresh on everyone's mind. One of the tanker navigators told me he was on leave when the Missile Crisis started, and he received an urgent telephone call directing him to return to his squadron "with all possible speed." The navigator said he was tooling up the Jersey Turnpike in his Mercedes at 110 mph when a highway patrolman pulled up beside him, saw the SAC sticker on his windshield, and waved him on. The word was out! This was a matter of national security, and the highway patrol wasn't going to mess with SAC crewmen. All available SAC aircraft were put on twenty-four-hour alert, and some aircraft were deployed closer to the expected action until the crisis was over. Later on, the story went around the squadron that the real reason Khrushchev "blinked" was because a SAC bomber, loaded with nukes, had flown up to a different point on the Soviet border every fifteen minutes during the Missile Crisis. That would have been enough to make anyone blink.

With this recent Soviet/Cuban threat in mind, it was easy to see why SAC took itself so seriously. Even when there wasn't an actual crisis in progress, about half of the SAC aircraft were constantly on alert. Everything was marked "Top Secret." SAC crews were continuously "authenticating" coded messages, and crews were tested and retested on the ground and in the air by the IG (Inspector General of the Air Force), CEG (Combat Evaluation Group), 2nd Air Force, and the local Standardization and Evaluation Board. On written tests, 90% was the minimum passing score for SAC crewmen, but the expectation was for crewmen to make a 100%. During actual training missions, inspectors were looking for the smallest error.

I soon learned all of this "readiness" training was nothing new for SAC crewmen. In many ways, SAC was still living under the shadow of its first commander, Gen. Curtis LeMay. Photographs of LeMay showed a mean-looking, cigar-chomping man with heavy jowls and a permanent scowl. Although he had retired from active duty a few years earlier, his legend lived on. It seemed that many of the SAC crewmen who knew him were more frightened of General LeMay than they were of nuclear war. LeMay was famous for firing anyone who displeased him, from numbered Air Force commanders on down.

One of the LeMay legends was about a young airman third class (a one-striper) who was guarding the flight line one dark night when an Air Force pickup truck approached his checkpoint. Remembering his training, the airman raised his arm and said, "Halt," but the truck continued to move forward. The airman unshouldered his weapon, and yelled, "Halt!" but the truck drove right on past him. At that point, the airman leveled his weapon and put a bullet through the rear window of the truck. The truck screeched to a halt, the door flew open, and out came a big black cigar followed by Gen. Curtis LeMay. LeMay marched up to the trembling airman, ripped the single stripe off his shoulder, and said, "That's for missing!"

In retrospect, with LeMay retired, the Cold War in stagnation, and Vietnam heating up, SAC's traditional nuclear deterrent role was already past its zenith when I joined SAC in 1966, but at the time, of course, we didn't know it. I did notice, however, the average age of SAC crewmen was older than I expected. Most of the crewmen were in their thirties, forties, and even fifties, and several men in their thirties were still flying as copilots. As a twenty-three-year-old supersonic T-38 pilot, I was initially unimpressed with many of these pot-bellied, chain-smoking, poker-playing "old men" who had been flying prop-driven airplanes when I was still playing in the sandbox. However, I had to admit some of them could tell great stories about places they had been and adventures they had lived through.

One of the first people I met when I reported in at the 917th Air Refueling Squadron was a tanker copilot named Brad Beck. Brad was a big guy with fresh scars on his face and hands. When I met him, he was still on sick leave from a freak accident which had nearly claimed his life. Brad, and the rest of his tanker crew, had been flying from Greenland to Alaska in the middle of an Arctic winter when Brad noticed a crack in the large, double-paned, side window just above his right armrest. Brad quickly fastened his lap belt, but not his shoulder harness, and was in the process of putting on his helmet when the window blew out! The aircraft, which was at an altitude of about 40,000 feet, completely depressurized in seconds and sucked Brad's head, arms, and shoulders out the window. The only thing that kept Brad from going all the way out was his lap belt. Brad's aircraft commander began an immediate emergency descent but then leveled off when he realized Brad would freeze to death even if he could get him to lower altitude where he could breathe. After several tries, the boom operator, M/Sgt. "Crash Axe" King, who was in danger of being sucked out himself, managed to overcome the force of the slipstream and pull

Brad's unconscious body back into the aircraft. Brad's helmet and gloves had been ripped from his body, and his nose had actually been blown over and frozen to the side of his face! Sergeant King dragged Brad into the back and got him on oxygen, but Brad was so near death when they got the plane on the ground in Alaska, the doctors didn't bother to individually wrap his frozen fingers. The Air Force flew Brad's wife up to Alaska to be at his bedside when he passed away, but he fooled them and got well. His only problem was that his frozen fingers had grown together as they healed, and a surgeon had to cut them apart.

My new aircraft commander, Capt. Billy Bird, who was full of stories, claimed he once had a bunch of Arab civilians build a cooking fire in the back end of his C-119 "Flying Boxcar" when he was flying Moslems from Khartoum to Mecca. Various crewmembers I met had served in Turkey, Spain, England, and Alaska, all very exotic-sounding places to me.

Larry, Ronnie, and Mike George (from left)—three brothers who all became Air Force officers. (Family photo album)

Consolidated B-36 bombers and North American F-86 "Sabre Jets" of the types which flew over Commerce, Texas, in the early 1950s. (USAF photos, National Archives)

Kaman H-43 "Huskie" Air Rescue helicopter and Lockheed T-33 "T-Bird" jet trainer of the types used for AFROTC flight indoctrination rides at Perrin AFB, Texas, during 1963. (USAF photos, National Archives)

Ron George after soloing his first aircraft, a Cessna 172, March 3, 1964. (Photo by instructor pilot)

Miss Barbara Hejl (the future Mrs. Ron George) and Cadet Maj. Ron George at the AFROTC Military Ball, East Texas State College, April 1964. (Photo by Jim Cross)

Grandfather Fred Ridley pinning second lieutenant bars on Ron at East Texas State University, January 1965. (Photo by Fred Bennett, Jr.)

Cessna T-37 "Tweety Bird" jet trainer of the type used in pilot training at Webb AFB, Texas, in 1965. (USAF photo, National Archives)

T-37 student pilots Ron George, instructor pilot Lt. Ron Castleton (in black hat), Bill Causey, and Robert Whitcomb at Webb AFB 1965. (Webb AFB photo)

Ron after soloing his first jet, a Cessna T-37, at "Woodpecker" auxiliary airfield, Colorado City, Texas, 1965. (Photo by instructor pilot Lt. Ron Castleton)

Class 66-G, Section FO, Webb AFB, with T-37 aircraft, 1965. Ron is second from the right. (Webb AFB photo)

Northrop T-38 "Talon" supersonic jet trainer of the type used in pilot training at Webb AFB, Texas, in 1966. (USAF photo)

Members of Class 66-G, Webb AFB, in T-38 formation flight. (Photo by classmate Bob Kusterer)

2nd Lt. Ron George with T-38 near graduation, Webb AFB, May 1966. (Photo by classmate John Geier)

Ron receiving his Air Force pilot wings and wife Barbara pinning them on, Webb AFB, May 10, 1966. (Photos by Fred Bennett, Jr.)

Boeing KC-135A jet "Stratotanker." (USAF photo)

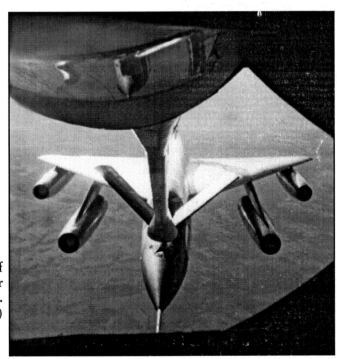

Aerial refueling of
B-58 "Hustler" over
Austin, Texas, 1967.
(Photo by author)

SAC alert crews responding to the Klaxon. (Dyess AFB photo)

KC-135 heavy-weight, water-injection, MITO takeoff. Imagine the forward visibility of the KC-135 pilot fifteen seconds behind the lead aircraft. (Dyess AFB photo)

Dyess AFB back gate and control tower during the 1960s. (Dyess AFB photos)

Dyess AFB flight line and commissary during the 1960s.
(Dyess AFB photos)

Dyess AFB hospital, where sons Robert and Jim were born (note tumbleweeds in the parking lot), and the base chapel, where we held the memorial service for the missing EWO. (Dyess AFB photos)

Lt. Col. Nick "The Greek" Itsines at Abilene, Texas, 1970.
(Photo by author)

Dyess AFB Tanker Crew R-112 aircraft commander Capt. Darrell
Dunlop. (Photo by author)

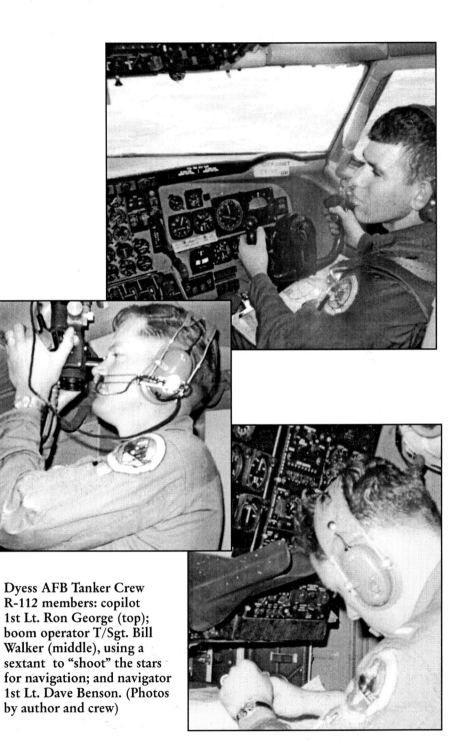

Dyess AFB Tanker Crew R-112 members: copilot 1st Lt. Ron George (top); boom operator T/Sgt. Bill Walker (middle), using a sextant to "shoot" the stars for navigation; and navigator 1st Lt. Dave Benson. (Photos by author and crew)

Scenes from Thailand, 1968: the Temple of the Emerald Buddha in Bangkok (top), and an elephant working teak logs. (Photos by author)

Scenes from Thailand, 1968: water buffalo (top) and spirit house.
(Photos by author)

Beach at Pattaya, Thailand. (Photo by author)

"Young Tiger" Headquarters—4258 Strategic Wing, U-Tapao Royal Thai Air Base, Thailand, January 1968. (Photo by author)

Top: Combat air refueling of F-105 "Thunderchiefs" over Southeast Asia during the 1960s. (USAF photo, National Archives)

Bottom: View from KC-135 cockpit in steep turn over the North Vietnam/Laotian border at the end of the "Young Tiger" combat air refueling mission, January 1968. (Photo by author)

B-52 on "Arc Light" bombing mission over South Vietnam during the 1960s. (Dyess AFB photo)

Contrails of KC-135s climbing to Flight Level 400 (40,000 feet) north of Luzon in the Philippines after refueling B-52s on "Arc Light" mission, March 1968. (Photo by author)

F-4 "Phantom" flying "MiG Cap" near the Korean DMZ (demilitarized zone) during the "*Pueblo* Crisis," March 1968. Note gun pod and "Sidewinder" missiles. (Photo by author)

Capt. Ron George, "youngest aircraft commander in SAC," May 1970. (Dyess AFB photo)

The 20th Year Reunion of Pilot Training Class 66-G, Webb AFB, held at Austin, Texas, August 1986. Pictured (from left) are Bob Kusterer, Fithian Shaw, John Ball, Ron Bandsuch, Paul "Tiger" Tiley, and Bill Stocker. (Photo by author)

CHAPTER 6

ALASKA

"The northern lights were running wild
in the land of the midnight sun."
Theme song from the movie *North to Alaska*

I had been in the squadron less than three months when
our first son, Robert Michael, whom we called "Bobby," was born
on November 23, 1966. Two weeks later, the squadron sent my
crew, R-112, to Alaska. Captain Bird was on leave, so the rest of
the crew went to Alaska with a very unusual aircraft commander.

Capt. Nick "The Greek" Itsines was a legend in SAC. He
was a handsome Greek bachelor, thirty-five years old, from New
York City. He also was an instructor pilot who knew more about
the mechanical systems of a KC-135 aircraft than any pilot I ever
met. What really made him famous, however, was that he was
totally unawed by SAC. Nick was always violating some petty
SAC policy or directive, and when he was called on the carpet,
he turned it into a joke and had everyone from the wing commander on down laughing about it. They would just shake their
heads and say, "Nick's done it again." All of this made Nick both
admired and envied by other pilots. For most of the younger
pilots, Nick was our squadron hero.

My first trip to Alaska with Nick was a real eye-opener. For
one thing, there was the weather. We were barely over Kansas
when we began to see snow on the ground and frozen lakes.
When we were over Nebraska, air traffic control reported we
were showing a ground speed on their radar of over 600 knots.

Since that was faster than a subsonic tanker aircraft was designed to go, we knew we had picked up a jet-stream tailwind. About the time we passed Saskatoon, Saskatchewan, I noticed another aircraft paralleling our course about 2,000 feet below us. After a while, I noticed the other aircraft changed course whenever we did, and it finally dawned on me I was seeing the shadow of our own aircraft inside the thin cirrus clouds below.

By the time we got to northwestern Canada, I began to see place names on the map, like Skagway, Whitehorse, and Dawson, which were right out of an old radio show called "Sergeant Preston of the Northwest Mounted Police." I looked for, but didn't see, the Mountie's famous wonder dog, "Yukon King." As I was looking down, however, I did see a jagged crack in a large frozen lake. I kept watching the crack and suddenly realized the crack was moving! It was a huge herd of caribou moving across the frozen lake.

When we got to central Alaska, the air was crystal clear. As we let down toward the Tanana River south of Fairbanks, we could see a large, gray-colored, dome-shaped object on the valley floor. Nick said the perfectly shaped "superdome" we were seeing was ice fog at Eielson Air Force Base. Nick said ice fog was created when moisture from aircraft and vehicle engines, the heating plant, and even people's breath froze and hung in the still air over the base.

When Nick rolled out on a long final approach, we could see about 1,000 feet of runway overrun sticking out from under the ice dome, but the base itself was completely hidden. As Nick was touching down, the weather instantly changed from VFR (visual flight rules) to IFR (instrument flight rules). We were on the runway and traveling at about 100 knots, but we could barely see the next stripe on the centerline. I was further amazed to see we had landed on about an inch of packed snow and ice! Nick brought us safely to a stop on the runway and then turned us right onto a taxiway by adding power on the left outboard engine. He showed me how the normal nose-wheel steering would simply skid on the ice. When he wanted to stop the turn, he brought up the right outboard engine. In this manner, we sort of waddled down the taxiway behind the "Follow Me" truck all the way to the parking ramp.

After we had completed the shutdown checklist, I went into the back of the plane and was getting my heavy parka out of my flight bag when our boom operator, Tech/Sgt. Bill Walker, opened the big cargo door beside me. A wave of incredibly cold air hit me in the face and instantly dried up the mucous membranes in my nose. I couldn't believe it was that cold. The local ground crew said it was 49 degrees below zero!

The ground crew timidly asked Bill if he had brought any fresh bread or vegetables with him. They were delighted when he produced a case of Mrs. Baird's bread and some green vegetables and fresh fruit. It was apparently a tradition for crews from "The Lower 48" to bring these coveted treasures to the frozen North. I suspect this small gesture guaranteed superb service for our aircraft.

The snow was about knee deep, and even on the sidewalks where most of the snow had been cleared, it squeaked under every step of our flight boots. Surprisingly, after the first initial shock, I was never uncomfortably cold in Alaska, but we didn't stay outside any longer than we had to. We wore quilted Dacron thermal underwear under our flight suits, heavy woolen boot socks, and a heavy coat with a wolf-fur parka. Wolf fur was used because the moisture from your breath wouldn't freeze on the fur. As we drove in, I noticed all of the parked vehicles were plugged into electrical outlets. The driver of the crew bus said the electrical cord was attached to a head-bolt heater, which kept the oil from freezing in the engine.

We were housed in a large, three-story, concrete building called "Ptarmigan Hall." It held a command post, crew lockers, sleeping quarters, mess hall, library, gift shop, movie theater, bowling alley, and swimming pool. The place was steam heated, and the pipes moaned and clanked. One night we had a small earthquake, which shook the windows and the steel bed frames.

I soon realized central Alaska had very short days during the winter months. In December the sun rose pale-yellow and cold around 1000 hrs. (10:00 A.M.), dribbled along the southern horizon, and then set behind Mt. McKinley (Denali) about 1400 (2:00 P.M.). The nights were long, cold, and dark, but starlight reflecting off the snow illuminated the world like faint moonlight. The stars themselves looked very bright and close. We saw an unusual number of shooting stars, or meteors, because the cold, dense air compressed the atmosphere inward near the poles and allowed meteorites to get much closer to the Earth before they began to burn up.

The incredible thing about an Arctic winter night, however, was the aurora borealis, or northern lights, which we saw nearly every night. The aurora borealis is supposed to be formed about 100 miles up in space when nitrogen particles in the ionosphere are bombarded by radiation from the sun. Sometimes the aurora looked like pale, lime-green, cirrus clouds blown like mares' tails before a cold front. At other times, the aurora looked like the bottom of a massive curtain or drapery with a very distinct lower edge that faded upward into nothingness. This beautiful pale-green, luminescent curtain might hang motionless for minutes or hours and then suddenly ripple like a curtain blown by a gentle breeze or a high wind. It was a fantastic, unforgettable sight. The aurora is supposed to be totally silent, but sometimes, on a still night, I swear I could hear faint static coming from this celestial visitor from outer space. On some night flights, the aurora looked so close we seemed to be flying through it.

Special care for aircraft was essential in Alaska. Aircraft brought from the Lower 48 and subjected to the intense cold of an Arctic winter dripped fluids from their hydraulic, fuel, and oil lines for several days until all the connections and fittings with their different coefficients of expansion and contraction had reached the same temperature. Once the aircraft was "cold soaked," the leaking stopped. Until then, the maintenance people really had their hands full.

When an aircraft part wouldn't work, the usual solution was to apply heat. The maintenance people had a heater cart with a large, flexible hose used to blow hot air into an engine or wherever it was needed. The aircraft cabin was usually icy cold during preflight, but one time our maintenance folks thought they would surprise us with a warm cabin. The only problem was they overdid it. Instead of everything in the cockpit being too cold to touch, everything was too hot! The heat was so intense a plastic writing tablet mounted above my right armrest melted and dripped down on my seat. That was the only time I was ever too hot in Alaska.

Jet engines actually perform much better at very cold temperatures because the air is denser, and the engine produces more thrust for the same throttle setting. A jet aircraft operating at minus 40 degrees F. uses only half the runway on takeoff that it needs on a 95-degree day. It was possible to even hear the difference in engine performance when watching a cold-weather, heavy-weight takeoff at Eielson AFB. Instead of the usual steady roar, there was a sharp, crackling sound like eggs frying in hot grease.

Our refueling missions out of Eielson usually took us northeast over the town of Circle, Alaska, across the Arctic Circle, over the Arctic Ocean and Banks Island, past the North Pole, and on to northern Greenland. We would fly for hours through the Arctic night and never see a sign of another human being. Once, however, I was startled to see a single lonely light shining in the darkness on the tundra below. At first I didn't believe what I was seeing, but when I looked again it was still there, probably a Defense Early Warning (DEW Line) radar station.

During these long flights, we could clearly hear Russian music over the HF (high frequency) radio and wonder about the Soviet enemy just a few hundred miles over on the other side of the Pole. We would eventually get to Thule, Greenland; refuel our B-52 bomber; and return to Eielson after seven hours in the air.

On one mission to Thule, we were warned our receiver aircraft might have difficulty getting out of its base in the northern U.S. due to a snow storm, and we would be expected to take its radio relay mission. Sure enough, about the time we got to Thule, we got an encoded message over the HF radio this had happened. We set up an orbit over Thule, flew around in circles for eight hours, relayed some radio messages, and returned to Eielson after fifteen hours in the air. We were so exhausted we just ate and dropped into bed.

Exactly eight hours later, our allotted crew rest was over, and we were rolling down the runway again for another fifteen-hour mission. About halfway through that mission, I was so tired I actually went to sleep, fell forward, and hit my head on the steering yoke. The plane was on autopilot, and it jerked a bit. Nick looked up, startled, and said, "Get in the back and get some sleep." The little fold-down bunk felt wonderful, and I slept for several hours, lulled to sleep by the constant roar of the jet engines. When Bill woke me up, Nick had me finish the flight and the landing on the glare ice back at Eielson.

On another occasion, one of our engines quit over Thule. We had to fly back across the top of the world on three engines, but we made it fine.

Other missions took us north from Eielson, over the Brooks Range, past Point Barrow, Alaska (where Wiley Post and Will Rogers crashed in 1935), and on across the Arctic Ocean to a refueling spot off the Soviet-controlled Severnaya Islands. There we met and refueled RC or EC-135 "weather planes," which were spying on the Russians. On some of these trips there was enough starlight for us to see a large, dark crack, as wide as the Mississippi River, where the snow-covered, frozen whiteness of the Arctic Ocean had split and then refrozen.

We thought we were going to spend Christmas in Alaska, but at the last minute we were told we would fly home on Christmas Day. This was, of course, good news, and Nick thought we should celebrate. Nick knew a couple at Eielson who were planning a Christmas Eve party, so he called them up and got our entire crew, including the boom operator, invited to the party. The Christmas cheer was flowing, and by 2200 hours (10:00 P.M.), it looked as though I might be the only one sober enough to fly out the next morning at 0600 (6:00 A.M.). About midnight, the other guests had left, and our hosts were hinting we should go home. Nick, however, didn't take the hint. He was still dancing to a recording of "Zorba the Greek" (and quite well, I might add) when we finally left the party at 0400 hours. We went back to Ptarmigan Hall, slept about thirty minutes, got up, preflighted the airplane, loaded up about twenty Air Force personnel who were returning to the Lower 48, and made an on-time takeoff at 0600.

Nick was doing the flying, and as he lifted off from Eielson, he said, "Gear up." So I raised the landing gear. He said, "Flaps up." So I raised the flaps. Nick then said, "You've got it," and he got out of his seat and went to the back. I didn't know what was happening. I thought at first he had forgotten something in his flight bag or maybe he was sick.

As we were climbing on out, I asked Bill what happened to

Nick, and he said, "He's asleep in the back." I guess Nick was paying me back for falling asleep over Thule. For several hours, I was really busy, flying the aircraft on autopilot, running the radios, changing the fuel panel, and trying to navigate. I put one of our crew chiefs in Nick's seat and told him to gently move the throttles back and forth as necessary to maintain our current airspeed (I suspect that crew chief is still talking about the time "he flew the airplane back from Alaska"). As we left Alaska and started down over the Canadian Rockies, we ran out of useable radio navigational aids.

Our navigator, Lt. Dave Benson, was asleep and slumped over his map table, so periodically I would have Bill wake Dave up to check our heading. Otherwise it was a beautiful winter day, and I just steered by the sun southward over British Columbia. I was too far from most UHF radio stations to give position reports, and I was having problems with the long-distance HF radio, so we went for more than two hours without a position report. About the time we got to Vancouver, air traffic control suddenly discovered we were "missing" and really gave me a bad time about the missing position reports. I thought they were going to write us up for a violation, but they finally calmed down about the time Nick got back in his seat.

We flew on down to Castle Air Force Base, California, dropped off some cargo and some of the passengers, and returned to Dyess AFB, Texas, where I penetrated the thickest layer of weather I had ever flown in and landed just about dark.

After we got the plane put to bed, I went on leave and drove to Dallas to spend a late Christmas evening with Barbara and Bobby at her folks' home in Lancaster, Texas. It was great to see them again, but it had been a long, long day.

CHAPTER 7

DYESS AIR FORCE BASE

"I wonder what was in that briefcase..."
Maj. Nick Itsines

Squadron life at Dyess quickly became a routine of sitting alert duty for three or four days straight, followed by "crew rest" (equal to half the time you were on alert), followed by either more alert or a training flight or two, and then back on alert. Alert duty got old in a hurry. It was like being in prison. I heard of one old sergeant who kept a six-inch steel bolt in the pocket of his flight jacket. Whenever he was on alert, he would, out of boredom, unscrew the bolt and then screw it back, over and over again, until he finally wore out the threads and could remove the nut from the bolt without turning it.

Alert crews worked, ate, slept, and killed time in a two-story, partially buried, concrete bunker known to SAC officials as the "Alert Facility," but to everyone else as the "Mole Hole." The first day of a four-day alert tour was devoted to preflighting the alert aircraft and to personnel briefings, training, and testing. The second day was devoted to mission planning for future training flights, and the third and fourth days you had to entertain yourself. SAC provided a small library, a chess board, a pool table, and a grade-B movie every night after supper. I did a lot of reading and pool playing, and many of the others played a lot of poker.

I recall sitting around one evening on alert with several young pilots, and we got to bragging about our landings. I said I could stand a cigarette lighter up on the glare shield and land so smoothly the lighter wouldn't fall over. The next guy said he could land so smoothly you wouldn't know the aircraft was on the ground until he set the brakes at the parking ramp and the aircraft rocked back and forth. The third pilot said, "You know what makes a really smooth landing? I like to come in and level off where the main landing gear wheels are just a quarter of an inch above the runway. Then I just hold it there until the air friction between the tires and the runway starts the wheels to turning. Once the wheels are turning at landing speed, I just e-e-e-ease the aircraft down that last quarter of an inch. The tires don't even smoke, and you get a really smooth landing." Well, nobody could top that story, so we all went to eat.

A small mess hall cafeteria in the Mole Hole provided surprisingly good food, including eggs cooked to order and steak at least once a week. Periodically, our experienced cooks would be shipped off to Vietnam or someplace, and we would all suffer as a new bunch of cooks were learning their trade. The alert crews would often complain about the chow like a bunch of spoiled school kids, but I noticed there was always a rush when the mess hall opened.

The three officers on a tanker crew slept together in a small room on the underground level of the Mole Hole. Many a night I would wake up to a small glow over in the corner and realize our aircraft commander was smoking in bed. It is a wonder he didn't set fire to the bedding and kill us all.

One of the most insidious features of alert duty was the Klaxon, an extremely loud noisemaker which sounded like a cross between an airhorn and the worst alarm clock you could imagine. At any time during an alert tour, day or night, the Klaxon could sound, and we were conditioned to react like Pavlov's dogs—except our salivation training was to run to our aircraft and start our engines.

If the Klaxon sounded while we were asleep, I got to where I would jump into my zippered flight suit, step into my zippered flight boots, and turn on the light switch (in that order) as I raced out the door. As we ran to the alert aircraft, we had to avoid running directly behind any of the other aircraft because the jet blast would roll you across the ramp and slam you into a blast fence.

The first pilot up the ladder and into the cockpit flipped the battery switch to "Emergency." The copilot glanced out the right window and shouted, "Clear on 4!" The aircraft commander placed the start selector switch into "Cartridge Start." A gallon-sized explosive cartridge in Number 4 engine ignited with a whistling roar, and clouds of black smoke rolled across the ramp as the engine wound up. Once Number 4 was started, the aircraft commander brought that throttle up to "Takeoff Power" (with the brakes locked) to supply bleed air through a duct in the wings to start the other three engines. While all of this was going on, the navigator was busy copying an encoded message which instructed us to either shut down the engines or taxi out and simulate a MITO (minimum interval takeoff).

A MITO was performed by having each aircraft cross the runway hold line exactly fifteen seconds apart. This procedure was designed to get all of the alert aircraft safely airborne and away from the base before it was hit by an incoming missile, but the dense clouds of black smoke from the aircraft ahead totally obscured all but the centerline of the runway, resulting in a blind takeoff.

We practiced actual MITOs from time to time, but for alert purposes we only got up to about 50 knots and then retarded the throttles and taxied back in and shut down. After that, the excitement was over until the next Klaxon sounded. This kind of conditioning is hard to overcome. Years after I left SAC, an especially loud alarm clock could still have me out of bed and running for my aircraft.

Once an alert tour was finally over, the aircrews would get to go home, visit with their families, and relax awhile. Many of my fellow crewmen would then go out and play golf with the same people they had been with on alert. I would go out by myself, or with my elderly friend, Mr. H. H. Hamilton, and hunt Indian arrowheads. At the end of our crew rest period, the others would have spent several dollars for green fees and lost golf balls, but I often had three or four perfect arrowheads to show for my efforts. I never did learn to play golf.

Although many pilots claim "Flying is hours and hours of sheer boredom punctuated by moments of stark terror," I found flying to be mentally and physically exhausting but always interesting. During training missions, I got to know Texas and the surrounding states pretty well from the air. Even at night, every city is distinct and can be recognized by its size and the location of lighted radio towers, airfields, major highways, and other features.

I recall one night when a cold front had just passed through, and the air was incredibly clear over Texas. We had just completed a refueling and climbed to Flight Level 330 (33,000 feet) just north of Houston when I noticed I could see Corpus Christi to the south, San Antonio and Austin to the west, and Dallas, Fort Worth, and Texarkana to the north. This, of course, was not so unusual; you can see a long way at high altitude on a clear night. However, as I looked again, I realized I also could see Brownsville in South Texas, Midland and Odessa in West Texas, and Lubbock and Amarillo in the Texas Panhandle. In fact, the only major Texas city I could not see was El Paso! I have never seen the air that clear before or since.

I don't recall ever flying a SAC mission exactly as planned. We frequently diverted around severe weather or had some mechanical problem. West Texas thunderstorms often towered to 60 or 70,000 feet, and we were under standing orders to avoid thunderstorms by at least twenty miles due to possible damage by hail and turbulence. Our flight safety officer showed us a photograph of a B-52 which had run into large hail in *clear air* nearly twenty miles from a thunderstorm. The B-52's nose and the leading edge of its wings looked as though the aircraft had been beaten thousands of times with a ball-peen hammer.

Once, on a night flight to Florida, we climbed above a mass of midlevel thunderstorms and flew for hours over clouds which continually glowed and pulsed below us like a boiling caldron of light. Twice on stormy nights I have seen St. Elmo's Fire dancing on our windscreen. St. Elmo's Fire is caused by static electricity and looks like clusters of little lightning bolts growing out of the corners of the windscreen. The little clusters of light would grow and nearly meet in the center of the windscreen and then die back to the corners again and again.

Radio or autopilot malfunctions were not unusual, and on

rare occasions we would lose power on one of our four engines. I recall at least three times we had to divert to another air base when someone had crash-landed on a runway ahead of us. Fortunately, no one was hurt.

On one flight, Nick the Greek and I dropped the new wing commander from Dyess AFB off at Barksdale AFB in Louisiana so he could attend a squadron reunion, and then we continued on with our mission. About three hours later, we were flying a navigation training leg over Kansas when we got an urgent HF (high frequency) radio call from the SAC Command Post. This was pretty unusual for a training mission; SAC usually reserved the HF radio for serious stuff. When I responded to the call, the Command Post officer, in a very concerned voice, said, "Is the colonel's black briefcase on board your aircraft?" We checked, and it was (it looked just like ours).

The Command Post officer then said, "You are hereby ordered to return to Barksdale immediately!" We were in the middle of a navigation training exercise we needed to complete, but we had been given a direct (and correctly authenticated) order from SAC, so we got emergency clearance from air traffic control to change our flight plan and fly direct to Barksdale. A few minutes later, the Command Post called back and asked our ETA (estimated time of arrival) at Barksdale. Whatever we said was apparently unacceptable, because we were ordered to "expedite" our flight.

Nick pushed our throttles forward until we were getting a "buzz" through the control column from near-supersonic air rushing over the curved portion of our wings. We made pretty good time across Kansas, Oklahoma, Arkansas, and Louisiana. However, as we descended through 10,000 feet and approached Barksdale, the local approach controller told us to slow down and enter a holding pattern for spacing with other aircraft in the area. Nick got on the radio and said, "Negative, negative, we have priority cargo; we must land immediately!"

Approach control said, "Roger, Roger, clear to land!" We were only three miles out on final approach and still moving at better than 280 knots when Nick finally chopped the throttles, raised the speed brakes, and had me lower the landing gear. We got on the ground safely and were met at the end of the runway by a staff officer, who whisked away the colonel's briefcase. When we were airborne again and everything had returned to normal, Nick said, "I wonder what was in that briefcase..." Our boom operator, M/Sgt. Bill Saunders, said, "I looked; it was the colonel's dress shoes he was going to wear to his reunion."

Tanker training missions were usually six to seven hours in length, and we were provided with a box lunch. There would be a choice of steak, chicken, or some other entree (all precut into bite-sized pieces) as well as two sandwiches, a boiled egg, a package of potato chips, pickles and olives, cheese and crackers, cookies, a can of juice, and some fruit. The boom operator would heat everyone's entree in the electric oven, and the whole lunch was quite tasty. There was more food in the box than I could eat, so I would take home the leftovers. When our son Bobby was about two years old, he began to associate my return from a flight with something good to eat. He wouldn't say anything, but he would meet me at the door with his little arms held out for the lunchbox. I have fond memories of those greetings.

CHAPTER 8

AIR FORCE
SURVIVAL SCHOOL

"You should never eat toads or fungi."
Survival School Instructor, 1967

In June 1967 I was sent to Air Force Survival School at Fairchild Air Force Base in eastern Washington State. All Air Force flight crew members were sent through this school to give them a better chance of surviving if they ever had to leave a disabled aircraft.

The school lasted about three weeks, and I had heard it was rough. The first week or so was devoted to classroom training on survival skills, physical conditioning, and "combative measures" which consisted of several kinds of martial arts combined with dirty street fighting. I wasn't real great at hand-to-hand combat, but I did learn several ways to kill an enemy silently and efficiently. I did well in the academic training and was asked to stand up in a classroom of maybe 200 students to be recognized as having one of the highest academic scores in the class.

We also learned how to maneuver a parachute by pulling on the risers, how to jump into a sandbox and land without breaking a leg, and how to get out of a parachute being blown across the parade ground by a giant fan. We also slid down a cable into a swimming pool, escaped from a parachute harness, swam out from under a floating parachute, and crawled into a one-man life raft.

Our instructors told us less than 5 percent of all air crewmen who go down at sea survive, but there is always an exception. They told us about one man who survived 275 days, by himself, in a one-man life raft. He had the "will to survive," which was the most important thing a downed airman could have.

Next came the night obstacle course. The obstacle course was traversed by crawling along on your hands and knees in the darkness, holding a small stick out in front of you to feel for coils of concertina wire and trip wires. When you found a roll of concertina wire, you rolled over on your back, lifted up the roll of barbed wire with your stick, and slowly crawled under the wire using your stick to lift the wire and dislodge the ever-present barbs.

There were instructors roaming around the obstacle course posing as the "enemy," and they would punch your ticket if they caught you making any noise or tripping a flare. I had been very careful, had felt a number of trip wires with my stick, and had successfully avoided the flares until right at the end of the course. All of a sudden, a flare popped right beside me, and I had never felt the wire. This escape and evasion business was tougher than it looked.

Immediately after the obstacle course, we were "captured" and herded into a mock prisoner of war (POW) camp. Much of what we saw there was classified, but it was the roughest day I had ever spent in my life. It impressed me enough to consider going down in a burning plane rather than being captured by the enemy.

The final part of the school was conducted in the Cascade Mountains about an hour's drive north of Spokane. We had been instructed for about a week in the making of shelters, backpacks, shoulder harness, ropes, and fishing equipment from parachutes. We were told we would be allowed to take only certain items and nothing else into the field. After we got off the bus, we had to open our packs for inspection, and any extra food or other goodies were confiscated.

For about three days, my unit of thirteen students was constantly with an instructor who showed us how to make fire with flint and steel, build shelters, find water, set snares, catch fish, and find berries. We also learned to smoke meat in a parachute teepee, signal search aircraft for help, navigate with a compass, and evade the enemy. Several of my classmates were concerned about being out in the forest at night. The lecture about bears had apparently made an impression on them.

The escape and evasion shelter I built under a deadfall in the forest was so well camouflaged I had trouble finding it myself when I took my instructor out to grade it. My instructor said I would have to take the first watch that night because no one else would be able to find my shelter to wake me up.

None of my classmates were from a rural background, and many of them had never seen a rabbit killed and prepared for cooking. We made a stew using all of the rabbit, including the heart, liver, kidneys, and lungs. My portion of the stew was served with a lung floating on top. It tasted okay, but the air sort of "squished" out of the lung when I bit into it.

Part of the training was to show us what it was like to be without sufficient food. I suspect all of us were really hungry for the first time in our lives. It was not a pleasant feeling. However, our instructors were right; the second day is the worst. After that, your stomach shrinks and you don't notice it as much.

For the final three days in the field, the students were broken up into two-man teams and given the task of navigating through the mountains and forests without being captured by the enemy. I was paired with a young airman second-class who was a good traveling companion. I was a first lieutenant at the time, and the airman looked to me for leadership. I guess this was my first real command in the Air Force.

On the next to the last day, the young airman and I were climbing a steep mountainside. It was about a 50-degree slope, and the only way we could make any headway was to pull ourselves up from one spruce tree to the next. I had developed a severe cold about two days before, and it was really sapping my strength. We finally sat down near the top of the mountain, heaving for breath.

After several minutes we recovered to the extent we could talk again, and the young airman turned to me and said, "Sir, would you like a candy bar?" With that, he reached into his pack and pulled out two English toffee Heath Bars and gave me one. I suppose I should have reprimanded him for having sneaked in unauthorized food, but that was the finest candy bar I have every eaten in my life! I have been addicted to Heath Bars ever since.

Later the same day, the airman managed to kill a spruce grouse with a rock. We dressed it and carried it with us, planning to cook it for dinner that night. However, we rendezvoused with "friendly guerrillas" that evening and had to contribute our spruce grouse to the community stewpot. I think I got a little taste of the grouse.

The next morning at daylight, "enemy" instructors attacked our camp, and we had to scatter amid automatic weapon fire. On the final morning, I got soaked and chilled crossing the last creek, but we had made it back to the waiting buses. We had not been captured during the entire field exercise, and we had found our way home. *We had survived!*

Later that day, back at Fairchild, they fed us a very welcome steak dinner, but my stomach had shrunk so much I couldn't eat it all. For several weeks after I returned from survival school, Barbara noticed I insisted on having a lot of food on the table. She also noticed I ate with my arms around my plate, like an animal guarding its food.

CHAPTER 9

TDY

"That sergeant can play his nose like a trumpet."
M/Sgt. Bill Saunders, Goose Bay, Labrador

As a copilot, I made a number of TDY (temporary duty) trips out of the Lower 48 with various crews. I made a total of three trips to Alaska, twice during the dead of winter and once during an unseasonably mild October and November when we hunted grouse and fished on the vast lands of Fort Wainwright. Twice we flew to Goose Bay Air Base, Labrador, where we pulled alert duty for fourteen days straight.

While we were at Goose Bay, my boom operator, M/Sgt. Bill Saunders, introduced me to a friend of his and said he was famous throughout the Air Force for his ability to play his nose. I thought at first Bill might be pulling my leg, and the other sergeant seemed very embarrassed when I blurted out, "Can you really play your nose?" However, with a little encouragement, the sergeant put both hands up around his nose and started playing "Reveille." He then switched to "Charge," "Taps," and several other well-known bugle calls. He could also play jazz trumpet numbers with the "Wah Wah" sounds. I still don't know how he did it, but it was pretty impressive.

There was a summer trip to Thule, Greenland, where we refueled B-52s for several days during a military exercise. As we made our first penetration and approach into Thule Air Base, we passed low over glistening white icebergs with their aqua-green, then aqua-blue, then violet-blue mass disappearing slow-ly into the deep, blue-black waters of the Arctic Ocean.

Thule sat in a deep box canyon which came right down to the shoreline. There was only one way in and one way out. The runway actually ran uphill, and a normal nose-high tanker land-ing resulted in a three-point touchdown at Thule. At the far end of the runway there appeared to be a huge gray cloudbank, but it turned out to be a glacier! Pilots made very careful landings at Thule because there was very little room for a missed approach.

As we taxied in, I saw an Arctic fox run across the taxiway, and other foxes were running around under the barracks which were built up off the ground on stacked timbers so that the heat of the buildings wouldn't melt the permafrost. Heavy curtains hung on the windows in the barracks so you could sleep in this "Land of the Midnight Sun." Down in the box canyon, the sun actually set behind the canyon wall for a couple of hours around midnight, but it never really got dark in August.

The debriefing officer told us, "There is a woman behind every tree at Thule, but there just aren't any trees." We found there weren't many other plants either. We could see some grass-es along the shoreline as we landed, but the only other plant life we saw on the entire base was a clump of grass someone had planted in a rock garden in front of the Thule Mess Hall. Tundra soils are fragile, and construction of the base years before had left Thule Air Base a sea of concrete, rocks, and grav-el which nature had not even started to reclaim.

One of my biggest TDY adventures as a tanker copilot, however, was around the world in another direction. In December 1967 we received orders to travel to Southeast Asia and participate in "Young Tiger" combat air refueling missions.

CHAPTER 10

SOUTHEAST ASIA

"Ship me somewheres east of Suez, where the best is like the worst,
Where there aren't no Ten Commandments an' a man can raise a thirst;
For the wind is in the palm-trees, and the temple-bells they say: 'Come
you back, you British soldier; come you back to Mandalay!'
On the road to Mandalay, Where the flyin'-fishes play,
An' the dawn comes up like thunder outer China 'crost the Bay!'"
From "Mandaly" by Rudyard Kipling

For me, the Vietnam Conflict was part mysterious East, part high adventure, and part terror. Our jet tanker crew flew twenty-eight combat missions and logged over 200 hours of combat air time over South Vietnam, North Vietnam, Laos, and the Gulf of Tonkin. We witnessed the Communist "Tet Offensive" in South Vietnam and were awarded the Air Medal and the Vietnam Service Medal, but at times the war had the unreal feeling of a vacation in the tropics.

Our aircrew, R-112, left Castle Air Force Base, California, on January 2, 1968. We rode as passengers aboard a KC-135 tanker flown by another crew and stopped briefly at Hickham AFB, Hawaii; Anderson AFB, Guam; and Kadena AFB, Okinawa en route to our final destination at U-Tapao (Ooh-ta pi o) Royal Thai Air Force Base on the Gulf of Siam in southern Thailand. Our crew included 1st Lt. Dave Benson as navigator, Tech/Sgt. Bill Walker as boom operator, me as copilot, and Capt. Darrell "Do Right" Dunlop as our aircraft commander. Captain Dunlop was a recent, and very welcome, addition to our crew. He was a slightly built, soft-spoken, prematurely balding Southern Baptist with freckles. He didn't look the part, but he was the best pilot I ever flew with in the Air Force. Darrell let me fly every other mission as the aircraft commander. It was another tremendous learning experience.

U-Tapao had been built only three years earlier by the U.S. Air Force in cooperation with the Thai government. There is a standing joke that the first thing the U.S. Navy builds when it builds a new airbase is the officers' club, but the first thing the Air Force builds is the runway. U-Tapao was a typical Air Force project. Air Force personnel were housed in primitive "hooches" (wooden-framed canvas tents) until the runways could be completed. However, the runways at U-Tapao almost didn't become operational at all due to an oversight.

There was a grove of tall "yang" or ironwood trees just off the north end of the runway. Since yang trees can tower over 200 feet in the air, it was obvious the engineers building the airbase planned to cut the trees before any aircraft used the runways. However, when a work crew was sent out to cut the trees, the local citizens were horrified. Trees in Thailand are living things and thus have spirits which cannot be molested. The construction engineers were in a panic. They had just built a 300-foot wide, three-mile-long concrete runway with accompanying taxiways and parking ramps which appeared unusable.

A meeting with local Thai officials was called, and the engineers asked if anything could be done. The Thais said they would check with the local Buddhist monks who were in charge of spiritual matters.

Sure enough, for a small fee, the Buddhist monks performed a ceremony in which they asked the spirits to come down out of the trees and enter a small carrying box. Once that was done, the box was moved to a new location, the spirits were released into other suitable habitat, and the trees were cut. Years later as a wildlife biologist, I would recognize this as a typical "trap and transplant" project.

By the time we got to U-Tapao, the runways were operational, the officers' club was built, and the crews were housed in new two-story concrete barracks. I was taking a shower in the barracks one day when I was surprised to hear an Oriental woman's voice in the bathroom. Surprise changed to alarm when I realized she was talking to me and pulling the plastic shower curtain aside! As it turned out, it was actually just two small Thai Boy Scouts with high-pitched voices trying to sell decorative pins. I was very relieved.

The officers' club was run by Americans but staffed entirely with Thais, from cooks to waitresses. We were briefed to never tip the waitresses more than a nickel because five cents in American money was equivalent to the Thai dollar or "*baht*" (a laborer's daily wage), and "throwing money around would destroy the Thai economy."

The food was usually the Thai version of American food, and it was fairly well prepared. However, I was surprised when a very delicious-looking chicken pot pie I ordered had all of the bones still in it. Another officer was even more surprised when his chicken and rice soup was served complete with about a dozen small cockroaches. The soup had been prepared from a dry mix which had been contaminated in shipment, but the cook apparently thought the dried cockroaches were just part of the ingredients. We always had limes in our iced tea, and I ate two slices of delicious, fresh, sweet, locally grown pineapple at nearly every meal. The pineapple cost five cents.

We traveled around the airbase on wooden benches in the back of small, canvas-covered, Japanese pickup trucks called "*baht* buses." Not surprisingly, the standard fare was one *baht*. Occasionally, we would ride a *baht* bus into the town of Sattahip about five miles away.

The big boys claimed Sattahip was "the dirtiest town in the Orient." I didn't know if that was true or not, but Sattahip sure had some foul-smelling open sewers along both sides of the streets. The sewers were covered only with loose-fitting concrete squares which formed the sidewalks. Down near the fish market, where the odor of rotten fish mixed with the odor of human waste rose up through the openings in the sidewalk, I had to walk out in the street to keep from gagging.

On our way back from Sattahip, we saw a road construction crew made up entirely of women except for a male foreman. Those dainty little women were all wrapped up in long shirts, baggy pants, and bonnets, and they were carrying crushed limestone in large wicker baskets. Each would fill up her basket, hold the two handles of the flexible basket together with both hands, squat down low to the ground, slowly work her wrists up over one shoulder, and stand up and stagger off with maybe 120 pounds of rock. I was impressed! I was even more impressed when I saw them fitting each of the small, jagged rocks together, one piece at a time, to form a smooth roadbed.

I have a lot of good memories of Thailand. The people were very friendly and seemed glad to have Americans in their midst. We always tried to speak to Thais we met on the street with a cheerful "*Sah wa dee*" (Hello). They would usually reply with "*Sah wa dee, Cup*" (Hello, sir).

I never saw anyone begging in Thailand, but they all seemed to have something to sell. I saw several food vendors selling small dried octopuses wrapped around a Popsicle stick. They had little pushcarts displaying clotheslines of drying octopuses. When you weren't looking, they would run up to you and stick that gruesome-looking, multi-legged, translucent-yellow thing in your face and say, "You buy? You buy?" Some of the fresh tropical fruits and vegetables we saw in the markets looked delicious, but we had been repeatedly cautioned about eating uncooked local foods which may have been grown or rinsed in contaminated water.

Even rather poor-looking, unpainted houses in Thailand usually had flowers growing in the yard, and the house itself was often half-covered in a massive bougainvillea vine bearing brilliant purple or fuchsia bracts, which made the whole place look like a tropical paradise.

Every house I saw in Thailand also had a spirit house, like a tiny Buddhist temple, the size of a birdhouse, on a pedestal out in the front yard. The spirit houses were lovingly maintained and decorated with colorful ribbons and offerings of food for the family's ancestors. The Thais said they tried to make the spirit house pleasing for their ancestors; otherwise the spirits would move back into the main house.

Buddhist temples with their distinctive, pointed roofs and bright colors were everywhere, and the sound of wind chimes from the temples was audible throughout the villages. We would see Buddhist monks with shaven heads and saffron-orange robes walking down the streets. We also saw children fishing in the "*klongs*" or canals, water buffalo grazing in the pastures alongside the road, and coconut palms and banana trees swaying in the breeze.

I read in the Bangkok English-language newspaper that banana trees were supposed to be the home of some unusual spirits known as "Banana Tree Dryads." The paper said if a man fell asleep under a banana tree, a Banana Tree Dryad would appear before him at night in the form of a beautiful woman. The dryad would then seduce him and begin to slowly steal all of his strength. After the first night, the man couldn't help himself; he would return night after night until his body dried up and blew away. The night after that article appeared in the paper, I noticed an unusual number of airmen sleeping under banana trees.

While we were at U-Tapao, we would swim in the surf of the Gulf of Siam right off the end of the runway. We also got to go to a resort town called "Pattaya," about an hour's drive away. Pattaya had luxury hotels, sailboats, good food, and German tourists. After seeing nothing but Oriental women for weeks on end, it was quite a treat to see those tall, blond, round-eyed German girls, even if they did have hairy armpits.

On one occasion we got to fly up to Bangkok on a C-130 "Hercules" cargo plane for a couple of days of R&R (rest and relaxation). We tried to stay in a luxury hotel operated by the U.S. Military known as "The Chao Phraya" (same as the river that runs through Bangkok). A room at the Chao Phraya cost $1 per night, but it was full. So we stayed across the street at the "Excelsior," a private hotel where we paid $10 a night (highway robbery!). From our balcony on the fifth floor of the Excelsior, we looked down and saw a Thai woman wading up to her neck in a sewage *klong* gathering watercress plants for food.

The next day we hired an English-speaking tour guide with a car and saw the sights of Bangkok. He took us to "Timland," where we saw elephants working teak logs, a native teasing cobras with his bare foot, and other natives dancing and kick-boxing. He also took us on a boat tour of the river, weaving in and out among oceangoing vessels and speedboats, past the Temple of the Dawn, through the famous Floating Market, and back to the King's Palace.

The King's Palace was a walled city that held fantastically beautiful buildings, including the Temple of the Emerald

Buddha and the palace which had been the home of the English teacher "Anna," immortalized in the musical *The King and I.*

Thais drove their vehicles as though the only controls were the accelerator and the horn. We saw one accident, and several near misses, at one traffic circle. Once we were riding in a taxi out in the country on a narrow, two-lane road when the driver saw we were concerned about his zipping in and out of oncoming traffic with only inches to spare. With a sly grin, he pulled his vehicle under the tailgate of a two-ton truck ahead of us which was traveling about 55 mph and drove for a while with the truck's tailgate only six inches from our windshield! When we protested, he pretended he couldn't understand a word we were saying (although he had spoken fluent English only a few moments before). When I got back to the States and Barb expressed concern about the way I was passing other cars, I would tell her, "Ten Thai taxi drivers could have passed in that distance."

Although much of Thailand seemed like a peaceful vacation spot, the large volume of military air traffic and the Thai soldiers with automatic weapons manning sandbag bunkers around the airbase quickly reminded you there was a war in progress only a few miles to the east. The Thais were very serious about security. It was rumored one Thai officer who caught a guard sleeping on duty simply shot the guard in the head as a warning to the others.

CHAPTER 11

COMBAT MISSIONS

"Yea, though I walk through the Valley
of the Shadow of Death, I will fear no evil.
For I am the meanest son of a bitch in the Valley."
U. S. military doggerel, Southeast Asia, 1968

I didn't feel very mean when we started out on our first combat mission in an unarmed aircraft loaded with more than 120,000 pounds of jet fuel. In fact, I had a bad feeling we would not return.

We left U-Tapao on a hazy January morning on a "Young Tiger" mission and flew north to "Red 1," a refueling route which began in northeastern Thailand. We rendezvoused on time with four U.S. Air Force F-105 fighter-bombers known as "Thunderchiefs" or "Thuds." These massive single-seat, single-engine, supersonic jet aircraft were painted in a green and brown camouflage pattern to match the jungle below. Each Thud was heavily loaded with rows of 750-pound bombs slung externally under their bellies. The gun port on their nose housed the 20mm Vulcan machine gun, which could fire 6,000 rounds per minute. Those Thuds looked mean!

With our Thuds in tow, we flew north and crossed the Mekong River into Laos at a speed of 320 knots and an altitude of 22,000 feet. Laos was supposed to be neutral, but the Communist Pathet Lao controlled most of the rural areas of Laos, and they had a reputation for killing and dismembering POWs. We now considered ourselves over enemy territory.

The Communists were armed with Russian-made, 37mm

anti-aircraft artillery (Triple A), which could reach 20,000 feet. All well and good, until you remembered some of those peaceful-looking, jungle-covered mountain peaks below us were more than 2,000 feet tall and a 37mm Triple A cannon could be transported on a reinforced bicycle. Worse yet, the more powerful 57mm cannon (which could be transported in a small truck) could reach 50,000 feet! However, we were too busy to worry about all of that as we continued to refuel each Thud in turn. As we approached North Vietnam, the Thuds slid off to the right, accelerated, and turned northeast toward Hanoi and "Operation Rolling Thunder." They were going "Downtown"!

Darrell bent our airplane around in a steep turn and headed for home. We had been briefed that if we had trouble and had to bail out of a disabled aircraft north of the Mekong, we should travel south through the jungle only at night and avoid all contact with local people. However, as we recrossed the Mekong back into Thailand, I realized we had survived our first combat mission. It was only three hours long. Nobody shot at us. It was a piece of cake.

On some combat missions we flew as a single tanker. At other times there were multiple tankers with each successive tanker flying one mile behind and 1,000 feet above the preceding tanker. Once when it was my turn to fly as aircraft commander, I led five tankers and twenty-four fighter-bombers (a total of twenty-nine aircraft) through a "mass gaggle" air refueling. I was busy for a while coordinating everything by radio among those twenty-nine aircraft and the air traffic controllers on the ground, but everyone knew their job and all of the refuelings were uneventful.

Air traffic controllers operating from radar units on the ground in Thailand or South Vietnam or on U.S. Navy ships in the Gulf of Tonkin were a tremendous help conducting air operations. For standardization, all of the air traffic controllers in Southeast Asia used the U.S. Navy terms "port" and "starboard" for "left" and "right" and "angels" instead of "flight levels" for thousands of feet of altitude. This meant U.S. Air Force crews had to learn U.S. Navy lingo, but we smugly thought whoever made that decision was probably right. It was undoubtedly easier to retrain Air Force than Navy personnel.

During daylight hours, there was often little visible evidence that a war was in progress. From our altitude, the green of the jungle looked unbroken except for an occasional clearing. Here and there, however, we saw the unmistakable evidence of a B-52 "Arc Light" bombing strike. The bombs left long, parallel lines of earthen craters in the green below. Some of the B-52s, also known as "BUFFs" (Big Ugly Fat Fellows), were flying out of U-Tapao. Others were coming out of Guam, hours to the east.

The BUFFs were dropping their bombs using radar navigation based on the best available intelligence, but their information was often twenty-four hours old, and it was hard to hit enemy troops moving around on the ground. Once, a B-52 crew really messed up and dropped their full bomb load one mile short of their assigned target. When word got back to Guam, the SAC chair-warmers were going to court-martial them, but then a message arrived from an U.S. Marine colonel who wanted those men decorated. He said the pinpoint bombing from that B-52 saved his unit from being overrun by a massive enemy assault. It was a strange war.

At night, we could see brush fires, like tiny red fingernail clippings, scattered on the blackness below. Sporadic magnesium parachute flares lit up the ground with white light, and fingers of red rocket fire streaking to the left and right marked the scene of ground warfare. We could also see the winking, greenish lights of Triple A as enemy gunners sought to bring down attacking American aircraft. Most of this activity was well below us.

One night, however, during the height of the Tet Offensive, we were headed eastward across South Vietnam, and there was an unusual amount of Triple A bursting below us. All of a sudden, as I glanced over to the left past Darrell, I saw a huge Triple A burst (probably 57mm) at our altitude. It is hard to judge distances at night, but I think the burst was a mile or more away. I don't think they were shooting at us, but it certainly got our attention! I recall thinking, *Lord, just let me live through this night.*

It seemed like the dawn would never come, but I glanced down at the instruments, and when I looked up, dawn was breaking across the Gulf of Tonkin. It was the most beautiful and welcome sunrise I had ever seen. I keyed the intercom mike and said, "And the dawn comes up like thunder out of China across the Bay!" I heard the boom operator's voice on the intercom say, "Copilot's quoting poetry again."

In addition to operational frequencies, we monitored the emergency radio frequency at 243.0 MHz known as "Guard Channel." One morning we had been briefed that an Air Force RB-66 loaded with radar-jamming equipment had been shot down west of Hanoi and two Air Rescue "Jolly Green Giant" helicopters trying to pick up the crew also had been shot down. Sure enough, later that day, we were refueling some Thuds, and we could hear some of the rescue operation over Guard Channel.

An Air Force A1-E single-engine, prop-driven, fighter-bomber aircraft whose call sign was "Sandy" was coordinating the rescue and trying to determine if it was safe to bring in a third helicopter. We could not hear anyone on the ground because they were equipped only with short-range, hand-held survival radios, but we could clearly hear Sandy as he tried to encourage those awaiting rescue.

Sandy would say, "Roger, Roger, understand I am passing directly over you. I can't see you for the undercast. Try to climb to higher ground." Then there was a pause, and Sandy said, "Uh, Roger, understand you have a broken leg." This one-sided conversation went on for some time, but finally Sandy said, "I'm low on fuel, but I promise I will be back here first thing in the morning." We could all imagine that poor guy with the broken leg preparing to spend the night in the jungle.

The next morning we were up flying again, and we heard the conversation continue, "Roger, Roger, understand I am directly over you. I can't see you for the clouds in the Valley. Try to climb to higher ground." Then there was a pause, and Sandy said, "Uh-h-h . . . Roger, understand you still have that broken leg." These conversations went on for the better part of a week, but Air Rescue eventually got some of those men out. Some of that story was written up in an article entitled "Air Rescue Behind Enemy Lines" published in the September 1968 issue of *National Geographic* magazine. I do not know, but I like to think, Captain Etzel, the man on crutches in the photograph on page 355 of that article, was the person on the ground who was talking to Sandy and who was rescued later that week.

On at least two other occasions, we were flying along minding our own business when we heard U.S. Air Force airborne radar controllers orbiting over the Gulf of Tonkin in E-121s report over Guard Channel the location of MiG fighters they were tracking over North Vietnam. Fortunately, we never saw any MiGs over Laos or Vietnam, but I can tell you it is very exciting to be flying an unarmed aircraft and *know* you are sharing the same airspace with enemy fighters.

After a little over a month at U-Tapao, we moved up to Takhli (Toc lee) Airbase north of Bangkok. Takhli was a fighter base. Instead of the 300-foot-wide runways I was used to, Takhli had runways only 150 feet wide. I was flying the aircraft on our first trip into Takhli, and when I rolled out on final approach, I could not believe I would be able to land a KC-135 on a runway that narrow. After all, the wings of a KC-135 are 130 feet long, and it looked as though our wing tips would be hanging over in the grass! But like a lot of things which look impossible, when you have to do it, you find out you can. It was just a matter of landing on the centerline of the runway.

Unlike U-Tapao, which had just been hacked out of the jungle, Takhli had been an airbase for a long time. Takhli had even served as a Japanese airbase during World War II when Japan occupied Thailand (then called Siam).

The Administration Building at Takhli, a white wooden structure with a green roof, also housed the base post office. The post office had a doorway so low I had to stoop to enter, even though I stood only 6'1 in my flight boots. The attic of the Administration Building had been designed as a pigeon loft, and pigeons were still living there. I suspect the ancestors of those pigeons once served as food for Japanese pilots.

There were at least two squadrons of F-105 pilots stationed at Takhli, and they were a wild bunch. Many of them wore long handlebar mustaches they had to fold when they put on their oxygen masks. I tried to grow a mustache while I was in Thailand, but my mustache looked sort of like a mouse on my lip, so I shaved it off.

When they were off duty, the Thud drivers wore unauthorized, brightly colored, handmade silk flight suits to the officers' club. One squadron's "formal" flight suits were royal blue and the other golden-yellow. They were gorgeous. These men were a cocky, confident, impressive-looking bunch of fighter jocks. They were good, and they knew it. They had to be to do what they were doing for a living.

Thuds always looked impressive, but a pair of Thuds, fully loaded, roaring down that narrow runway, side by side, for a night combat mission, with their engines shaking the flight line and the red-orange flame cones from their afterburners nearly doubling the length of their aircraft, were awesome to behold!

Sometimes we would lead a flight of four or five F-105s from Takhli to one of the refueling areas over Laos, top off their tanks, and then pick up other fighters returning from their targets and refuel them on the way home. For one of these outbound legs, we were at the end of the runway with our receivers (five Thuds with the call sign "Victor Flight"). As we watched, the Thud crew chiefs standing on the ramp armed the bombs, showed the safety pins to the Thud pilots, snapped to attention, and saluted warriors they might never see again.

Darrell shoved our throttles forward and began our takeoff roll with our fighters right behind us. We got our aircraft safely airborne and were climbing out in a gentle right turn waiting for the Thuds to join on our wing when we heard Victor Lead order, "Victor Flight, check in." Two said, "Toop." Then there was a long pause, and finally Four said, "Uh, I think Three went in on takeoff." There was another long pause, and Lead said, "Spare, join up on Two."

At first, we couldn't believe what we had heard, but after we got back from the flight we were told Victor Three had an engine failure on takeoff and had crashed with a full bomb load under his belly. Amazingly, the pilot had ridden the concussion forward in what was left of his cockpit and had survived the accident. Unfortunately, the accident had shaken him up mentally. He thought he had been shot down for a second time over North Vietnam. This was apparently more than he could take. When we left Takhli two weeks later, the injured pilot was still in the hospital and still unsure of where he was. I hope he recovered.

Several months before we got to Takhli, another Thud pilot with a dead engine was more fortunate. When we got to Takhli, people were still talking about the incredible emergency refueling which saved his life. According to the story, two Takhli Thuds with the call sign "Brome Flight" were trying to coordinate the rescue of one of their fellow Thud drivers who had been shot down over North Vietnam. Things were not going well, and they had to stay long after their fuel gauges said it was time to go. After several tries, they made radio contact with a tanker, which raced north to meet them. However, just as they made visual contact, Brome Two's engine flamed out due to fuel starvation.

Brome Lead asked the tanker for a "toboggan" (a descending air refueling). Brome Two, with the dead engine, was able to coast in behind the diving tanker, and the boom operator locked on to him in one try. The locking mechanism held like a vise, and the tanker dragged the Thud southward until they got enough JP-4 into him for a restart. Brome Two then slid over so Brome Lead could refuel, and they all made it back safely. A firsthand account of this remarkable refueling was later published in the book *Thud Ridge*, by Col. Jack Broughton, the pilot of Brome Lead.

Whenever a Thud driver completed his tour of 100 combat missions, it was a time for celebration. As he returned to base, the lucky pilot would call the control tower and request clearance for a "100-mission pass." The tower would clear all of the other aircraft out of the traffic pattern, and the Thud would come screaming in just off the deck at about 500 knots. When he crossed the field boundary, he would light his afterburner, pull up into a spectacular climb, do some slow rolls, make a final zip around the pattern, carefully complete his final landing, and then have a big party at the officers' club before being rotated back to the States.

One morning we were holding just short of the active runway at Takhli completing the "Before Takeoff Checklist" when Darrell noticed an engine instrument fluctuating slightly. Darrell got clearance from Takhli Tower to run up the engine for a maintenance check, but Tower said to watch out for a crew of Thai construction workers who were repairing the taxiway behind us.

Since visibility from the cockpit toward the rear of the aircraft was limited, Darrell gently turned the aircraft so our jet blast would be away from the workers and toward some small trees off to the side of the taxiway. However, when Darrell brought the throttle up, I glanced back and saw a dozen water bottles and some lunches wrapped in banana leaves and paper go flying through the air behind the aircraft. The lunches had been stored in the tree branches for safekeeping, and we had not seen them. I hope those workers eventually forgave us for messing up their lunches.

On another takeoff from Takhli, Darrell was flying and I was adjusting the throttles to "Full Military Power" by setting the engine pressure ratio (EPR) gauges to a reading of 2.83. About the time we went through 120 knots, I heard the boom operator's voice over the intercom say, "Check Number 4." I quickly rechecked Number 4 engine, and it was showing an EPR of 2.83, just as it should, so I replied, "It's okay." Bill's voice went up an octave, and he said, "Check fuel flow on Number 4!" When I glanced back down at the fuel flow gauges, I was horrified to see the fuel flow on Number 4 was far below the other three engines! The EPR gauge was malfunctioning, and I had been slowly pulling the power back on Number 4 to make the EPR gauge read correctly. I quickly shoved the throttle for Number 4 back up with the others as we continued to accelerate down the runway.

All of this conversation and jockeying with the throttles had understandably caused Darrell some concern, and he took his eyes off the runway and was looking down at the gauges to see what was wrong. At that moment I glanced up and saw we had run out of runway. I screamed, "Rotate," and Darrell hauled back on the control column. Darrell got the nose wheel off the ground, but the main landing gear wheels hit the fighter tail hook cable lying flat across the far end of the runway. There was a little bump, and we completed the takeoff in the overrun. No mechanical damage done, but it nearly caused heart failure in four tanker crewmembers. Without Bill's help we might have run off the end of the runway without ever reaching takeoff speed. Another valuable lesson learned: *Trust your instruments, but check them all.*

Most of our missions over the Gulf of Tonkin involved the refueling of F-4 "Phantoms," rather than F-105s. F-4s were big, powerful, twin-engine jet fighter-bombers, so ugly they were pretty.

We were headed north up the Gulf over international

waters one day to meet our F-4s coming out of North Vietnam when I looked down to the right and saw two jet contrails rising out of the huge land mass of Hainan Island. As I watched, the contrails continued to climb rapidly upward on an intercept heading to our aircraft. There was reason for concern, since Hainan Island belonged to the People's Republic of China, and China and North Vietnam were supposed to be allies. We were all alone in an unarmed aircraft, and these contrails were likely coming from Chinese MiG-19 fighters! As I continued to watch, the contrails suddenly ceased.

The MiGs, if that is what they were, had apparently flown into a different thermal layer, and we now had no idea where they were. After an anxious minute or so, the contrails resumed, but now they were headed back toward Hainan Island. At the debriefing after the flight, I told the Air Force Intelligence Officer (an oxymoron) what I had seen. He pooh-poohed the idea they were MiGs. However, years later, I met an EC-135 crewmember who had been intercepted by Chinese MiGs over the Gulf of Tonkin at about the same time we were there.

On a later mission over the Gulf of Tonkin, we were orbiting over international waters off Haiphong Harbor, just beyond SAM (surface to air missile) range, waiting for a "Wolf Pack" of F-4s which had been hunting "Red Bandits" (MiG-17s) and "Blue Bandits" (MiG-21s) over North Vietnam. When the F-4 flight came up on our refueling frequency, the flight leader called for a fuel check. Two, in a confident, professional voice, said, "Toop, 2,000" (indicating he still had a ton of fuel on board). Three said, "Threp, 1,500," and Four, in a young, terrified, high-pitched voice said, "I'm out of fuel!" Almost instantly, the radio was overwhelmed with horrible static as the North Vietnamese jammed the radio frequency in an attempt to prevent the refueling of the fuel-starved F-4.

This was really a critical situation. Since we had not made radio contact with the F-4s prior to the jamming, we didn't know whether we were north or south of them. The worst thing we could do would be to guess wrong. Darrell put us in a 60-degree bank turn so at least we would not be going away from them. Darrell was spinning us around in one spot, hoping the F-4s could find us with their powerful intercept radar, Dave was running his radar transponder, and Bill was on his belly in the back. I was watching for aircraft when suddenly one of the F-4s came from behind and passed about 100 feet in front of our windscreen (just to let us know they had arrived). At the same time, over the intercom, we heard Bill's voice say, "He's hooking up!" Almost instantly, the yellow "boom engaged" light on our instrument panel came on. I flipped on two air refueling pump switches and said over the radio, "He's taking fuel." A second or two later the jamming ceased. I guess the North Vietnamese figured the F-4 had gotten away.

Ever so carefully, Darrell rolled us back into straight and level flight and headed us south toward home. Those F-4 jocks acted as though 60-degree bank refuelings were routine to them. It was the hairiest refueling I ever saw.

We stayed on in Thailand for an extra week, so Bill could receive an extra reenlistment bonus for reenlisting in a combat zone. Our crew was then sent to Kadena Air Base, on the Island of Okinawa, where we had some more adventures. In some ways, Kadena Air Base was like returning to the States. The food was excellent, we had lemons (not limes) in our iced tea, and the military housing was much less primitive. However, the sight of World War II Japanese pillboxes moldering in the undergrowth, bamboo construction scaffolding on tall buildings, and native farmers tending their crops between the taxiways sure didn't look like the States.

Our missions out of Kadena usually took us just north of Luzon in the Philippines, where we refueled B-52s on Arc Light bombing missions to Vietnam. Once we completed our refueling, we turned back to the northeast toward Kadena and climbed to Flight Level 400 (40,000 feet) for optimum fuel efficiency.

This usually put us back at Okinawa with minimum fuel, but that generally wasn't a problem. However, as I made our descent into Kadena one day, the windscreen anti-ice on Darrell's side failed. The combination of a super cold tanker just down from the stratosphere and the high humidity over the Pacific Ocean created about a half inch of opaque rime ice on the inside of Darrell's window. The ice, which looked like the inside of an old refrigerator, would reform faster than Darrell could scrape it off. We didn't have time to troubleshoot the prob-

lem or fly around until the aircraft warmed up; we were at minimum fuel. Darrell said for me to just continue the approach,
and I made an uneventful landing. It was only after I heard Bill
say, "Well done, copilot," that I realized what a fix we would have
been in if the anti-ice on both windows had failed.

While we were at Kadena, we were trained to refuel the
Lockheed SR-71 "Blackbird" (or "Habu"). The Habu was a
Mach-3, exotic-fuel spy plane which was also stationed at
Kadena. We never did actually refuel a SR-71, but once, over the
Gulf of Tonkin, we met a contrail coming out of China at
extremely high altitude and airspeed. We suspected it was a
Habu returning from a photo surveillance mission of the
Chinese mainland.

I recall one other unusual mission out of Kadena. We were
sent north to Japan and then northwest to Korea to refuel some
aircraft involved in a classified mission to obtain information
about the crewmen of the U.S. Navy spy ship, the *Pueblo*, which
had been illegally captured in international waters by the North
Koreans several weeks before. The *Pueblo's* crewmen were eventually released, and our tanker crew was awarded the Armed
Forces Expeditionary Medal for our participation in that action.

On our way back to the States, again as passengers on a KC-
135 flown by another crew, we stopped off for fuel and passengers at Hickam Air Force Base in Hawaii during the night and
departed before dawn. I could now brag I had seen Hawaii
twice, both times during the middle of the night.

When we got to California and I was able to call Barbara,
one of the first things she said was, "Bill Causey's plane is missing, and the crew is presumed dead." Causey, one of my best
friends from pilot training, dinged on a nighttime, low-level, B-
52 training mission over the Gulf of Mexico just off the Texas
coast. His aircraft simply disappeared off the controller's
radarscope. Although some wreckage washed ashore on
Mustang Island, none of the bodies was ever recovered. I got
back to Texas in time to attend Bill's memorial service at
Carswell Air Force Base in Fort Worth.

After all that my crew and others I knew had been through
in Southeast Asia, it was hard to imagine we had lost Causey on
a stateside training mission.

CHAPTER 12

MAYDAY, MAYDAY, MAYDAY

"Aviation in itself is not inherently dangerous.
But to an even greater degree than the sea,
it is terribly unforgiving of any
carelessness, incapacity, or neglect."

Caption under an old photograph of
a biplane stuck in the top of a tree

After we got back to the States and resumed "safe" stateside training missions, I was reminded once again how quickly things can go wrong. Crew R-112 had completed its assigned refueling and navigation leg over eastern Colorado, and we were headed home to Abilene, Texas. It was a beautiful afternoon, the weather was clear, and the visibility was greater than fifteen miles. We were just north of the Amarillo VORTAC Station southbound at FL 380 when I saw a thin, black exhaust trail and a tiny dot coming from the east. It looked like it might be a fighter that would pass Amarillo less than a half mile ahead of us.

As I watched, the fighter suddenly turned right, met us head on, and grew in size at an alarming rate! I suspect that naval aviator was as alarmed as we were because he jerked back on his stick, and a Navy F-8 "Crusader" shot by only fifty feet over our heads. We were so close, we could clearly see the pilot's face! After Darrell and I could breathe again, Darrell got on the radio and reported a "near miss" to Fort Worth Center.

Center came right back and said that wasn't possible because the fighter was 1,000 feet below us. There was total silence over the radio when Darrell told them the fighter had passed over, not under, us. Later, a playback of the voice tapes

75

revealed Center had assigned the Crusader to the same altitude we had been assigned. Only clear weather and that fighter jock's reflexes had saved our lives. If we had been in the soup, we would never have seen each other in time. *That was the closest I ever came to being killed in the Air Force.* We would not have had time for a Mayday call.

I heard my first Mayday call when I was a still a student pilot, flying solo, and leading a two-ship formation of T-38s out of Webb Air Force Base. My earphones crackled, and I heard a young, high-pitched voice on emergency Guard Channel shout, "Mayday, Mayday, Mayday, Tango Two, F-100, Cannon Air Force Base, flameout (an engine failure), 20,000 feet!"

An older, deeper, more-authoritative voice (obviously Tango Two's instructor pilot in another F-100 jet fighter), sounding somewhat bored, said, "I'll read you the checklist." The IP then read, "Throttle cut off, ignition switch off, fuel select reset, throttle to air start, ignition switch on" and several other steps. The IP then said, "Well?"

The student, now in a much calmer voice, said, "Negative relight, sir." The IP's voice rose a full octave, and he said, "I'll read the checklist again!" The IP went rapidly through the checklist, and when he had finished, the student, in a very confident voice, said, "Negative relight, sir, I'll try it again."

The instructor's voice rose another full octave, and he screamed, "Negative! Negative! I am ordering you to bail out now!" The student, in a deep, confident voice, said, "Roger, sir, bailing out." After only a few seconds, the instructor, his voice now almost normal, announced to Air Traffic Control, "He's standing by his burning plane. He's waving. He's OK."

I've always thought this incident offered an unusual study in human behavior. The student, apparently thinking that as long as he went through his procedures he would be all right, grew progressively calmer to the point of totally ignoring the danger. The instructor, once he recognized this was not going to be a normal relight, became more and more concerned, and finally ordered, in a near-hysterical voice, the only option left with only seconds to spare.

The only other time I heard a Mayday call, we were flying over the Canadian Arctic in a KC-135 when we heard over the

HF radio, "Mayday, Mayday, Mayday, Lima 17, B-52, 21 degrees north, 122 degrees east, our E-Whoa (EWO, or electronics warfare officer) has bailed out!" The radio call was so clear we figured it had to be close by, but when our navigator plotted the coordinates, Lima 17 was just north of Luzon in the Philippines, about a fourth of the way around the globe. We were just getting an incredible radio wave bounce.

Lima 17 talked to someone for a while, but we did not hear any more of the incident until we got back home to Dyess Air Force Base. As it turned out, Lima 17 was from our home base. Lima 17 was about to hook up for an air refueling at the time of the incident. The B-52 was wallowing around some in the air, and the boom operator called an emergency breakaway. The EWO (who doesn't have a window to look out), apparently thought they were in danger of a midair collision so he bailed out. His parachute opened okay, but he had bailed out over a typhoon!

The seas were too rough to attempt a rescue. The emergency radio beeper in his one-man life raft was heard for two days, and then it was heard no more. No trace of him was ever found. We held a memorial service for him at the Dyess Air Force Base Chapel.

CHAPTER 13

MOVING UP AND WINDING DOWN

"You are probably the youngest aircraft commander in SAC since World War II."

Col. James Stanton, Squadron Commander, 1969

Except for occasional moments of stark terror, my Air Force career after we returned from Southeast Asia was fairly routine. I was promoted to instructor copilot and was assigned to a "Standboard" (Standardization and Evaluation) crew. Nick "The Greek" Itsines, now a major, was again my aircraft commander. I was now one of the "bad guys." I didn't give actual check rides in the air, but I gave written tests and simulator check rides to air-crews. The simulator was like the cockpit of a KC-135 mounted inside a railroad car. Twice a year, the simulator car would be shipped to Dyess, and I would give simulator training rides and tests to all of the pilots and copilots. The good part about being on a Standboard crew was that I didn't have to pull alert duty as often.

I was on alert, however, the day a man I'll call "Major Johnson" went crazy. The first indication that something was wrong was when we noticed Major Johnson actually asking ques-tions and taking notes at the Sunday morning alert briefing. This was pretty unusual in itself, but the questions Major Johnson was asking were about the time hack, the perfectly clear weather, and other trivial matters. Everyone looked at each other and rolled their eyes like, "What's this all about?" Later that day, the Klaxon sounded, and everyone rushed out to their aircraft—everyone, that is, except for Major Johnson.

Major Johnson broke down crying. He said later he thought it wasn't just an exercise, that we were actually going to war, and his family would be killed by the incoming nuclear attack from the Soviets. Major Johnson had been involved early in his career with the hydrogen bomb tests on Bikini Atoll in the Pacific, where he flew B-29s under radio control directly into the nuclear cloud. He had seen firsthand what an H-bomb blast could do.

The squadron commander asked Nick and me to give Major Johnson and his crew a check ride in the KC-135 simulator, which happened to be in town. Major Johnson promptly "crashed" during the first emergency situation, and the squadron commander took Major Johnson off alert duty and placed him on a desk job. Over the next several weeks, as we observed Major Johnson working at his 8:00 to 4:30 desk job while we were on alert twenty-four hours a day for four days straight, we began to wonder who was crazy.

Even as a Standboard crew, Nick and I were still subject to no-notice inspection flights whenever we flew. On one no-notice Combat Evaluation Group check ride as Nick's copilot, I received a "Highly Qualified" rating, something SAC pilots or copilots seldom received. Along about that same time I was promoted to the rank of captain and given a "regular," rather than a "reserve," Air Force officer's commission. This was quite an honor. It meant my aircraft commander and my squadron commander thought I would make a good career officer.

Time passed, and our second son James Russell, whom we called "Jim," was born on April 22, 1969, while I was in the process of upgrading to aircraft commander. As usual, I had trouble with instrument flying, got too high on my instrument approach, and flunked that portion of my upgrade check ride. Very embarrassing! However, they let me retake the ride a month later, and I passed it fine. My squadron commander, Colonel Stanton, said I was probably the youngest aircraft commander in SAC since World War II!

In the fall of 1969, I was given my own crew, R-111. My copilot was Capt. Robert Goodenough, the navigator was 1st Lt. Jack Sturgeon, and the boom operator was M/Sgt. Herman Bradix.

Shortly after I was given this new crew, we were headed west toward El Paso when we began to pick up "CAT" (clear air turbulence). CAT is sometimes encountered near the transition between a jet stream and slower-moving air. I had the airplane on autopilot, and the CAT started with just a little tremor barely visible in the steering yoke. This small movement rapidly grew until the yoke was traveling full swing left and right and banging against the stops. The whole aircraft was shaking violently. I was too scared to try to take the plane off autopilot and hand fly it, and I literally could not force myself to look out the window at the wings. I was afraid they were about to snap off or at least shed their engines.

We were too heavy to climb to a higher altitude, so I descended and slowed down. Nothing helped. Our receivers, a bunch of fighters out of Luke Air Force Base, were waiting for us over Arizona, and we just pressed on through nearly 100 miles of the worst turbulence I had ever seen. All I can say is that it is a good thing Boeing makes sturdy aircraft.

On one of my flights as a new aircraft commander, I flew my aircraft to FL 440 (44,000 feet), higher than I had ever flown before. We were trying to fly a navigation training leg, but the boom operator was having trouble finding the sun in his sextant because of a thin layer of cirrus clouds. I kept climbing and climbing, but we never got to the top of the cirrus. Although the visibility was much better at FL 440, I had the KC-135 so near its operational service ceiling it was kind of wallowing around in the air, and the boom operator never got a usable fix. We had to finish that navigation leg on another flight.

As the newest aircraft commander in the Wing, I got more than my share of no-notice check rides and inspections by all sorts of people, but we generally made it fine. The only real problem I had was with a full colonel I'll call "Colonel Smith." Colonel Smith (who was trying to make general) was a large man who was always whirling around and stumbling over his own feet, much like President Gerald Ford several years later. Because of this habit, the enlisted men, behind his back, called him "Dancing Bear."

One day my crew was participating in a SAC exercise, and we were expecting a Klaxon and a simulated MITO. To save taxi time, Colonel Smith issued an order over the command post radio directing all the alert aircraft to start their engines, move up from their dispersed parking areas, and park single file on the taxiway leading to the main runway. He then ordered us to shut down our engines and await the Klaxon.

Knowing I was the youngest aircraft commander in the squadron, Colonel Smith singled me out and ordered me into position as the first tanker. Although we were all closer to the runway, the problem with this arrangement was that any aircraft that was slow in getting started blocked all of the aircraft behind it. Sure enough, when the Klaxon sounded, my cartridge fired okay, but I couldn't get enough bleed air out of Number 4 engine to bring all of the remaining engines up to start speed. Following proper procedures, I cut out the slowest engine, started the other two, and then had to wait until the slow engine coasted to a complete stop before I could reengage the starter (reengaging the starter while the engine was turning would shear the starter shaft).

In the meantime, Colonel Smith was on the radio demanding to know what was going on and offering all kinds of advice. I was eventually able to move forward, and we all crossed the runway hold line within the required time limit. The colonel, of course, took full credit for our success at the debriefing.

The colonel was always trying to improve things by issuing new operating orders. Ever since I had been in SAC, the standard procedure for aircraft taxiing back into a congested parking area was to stop the aircraft and let the navigator and boom operator get down on the ramp to serve as "wing walkers" to signal the pilots if the wing tips got too close to another aircraft or a blast fence. Colonel Smith changed all of that by issuing a written order which stated that from now on the correct procedure would be to radio the Command Post and ask for Maintenance to send some wing walkers out in a truck. He was the senior officer; if that was what he wanted, fine with me. However, less than two weeks after that order was issued, I was taxiing back into the parking area after an alert, and there were no wing walkers in sight. Following the newly published orders, I stopped my aircraft and called the Command Post for wing walkers.

Almost immediately, a dark blue Air Force staff car raced out from behind a blast fence and parked directly under the nose of my 297,000-pound aircraft. Colonel Smith's voice came over the radio from the staff car, saying, "What's the matter, George?" I responded, "Sir, I need wing walkers to safely enter the parking area." Colonel Smith responded in a very sarcastic voice, "Did you ever think about letting your navigator and boom operator off to serve as wing walkers?" I was speechless; I wanted to say, "Did you ever think about reading your own orders?" but with the whole base listening, I didn't think that would be very good for my Air Force career. Suddenly, I had an inspiration and said, "Sir, I will brief you when I get on the ground." By this time, I had Maintenance trucks coming from everywhere and more wing walkers than I could possibly use.

Colonel Smith backed his staff car out of the way. I parked my aircraft and then walked down the ramp toward the colonel's car. By the time I got there, several senior aircraft commanders were standing around the car, and they had apparently reminded the colonel of his own orders because he was looking a little sheepish. I walked up, saluted, and said, "Sir, I'm sorry I always seem to be messing up." He waved me off with, "Uh, that's all right, that's all right," but he never acknowledged he had made a mistake.

A month or so later, there was a New Year's Eve party at the officers' club. I was on alert and didn't go, but I wish I had. Colonel Smith appeared on stage that evening as "Baby New Year," dressed only in a sheet folded and pinned around him like a huge diaper. To complete the image, he swung his hips and waved his arms to the music, "You Must Have Been a Beautiful Baby."

Unknown to the colonel, someone stepped out on the stage behind him dressed in a bear suit (remember "Dancing Bear"?) and began to wave its paws and swing its hips just like the colonel. The audience was howling with laughter; some people were actually rolling on the floor. The colonel's act was the hit of the party, but not in the way he envisioned. As he completed his number and began to turn around, the bear quickly moved out of sight. It wasn't until later, when the colonel's wife asked, "What was the bear suit all about?" that he knew he had been had. He was absolutely furious!

The next day he ordered everyone he saw to reveal the identity of the person in the bear suit. No one ever did. In some ways, it was kind of sad to see him the laughingstock of the base.

About that same time, I had a decision to make about my own Air Force career. I had now completed four and a half years of my five-year Air Force commitment. I had a lot going for me. I was an Air Force captain with a regular commission. At twenty-six years of age, I was one of the youngest aircraft commanders in SAC. I had my own combat aircrew on a $5 million KC-135 aircraft. I was, as we claimed, "The president of a $5 million corporation."

On the other hand, I had always been sort of a civilian in military uniform. I had seldom lived on base. I had never learned to play golf or poker or even drink coffee. I didn't live and breathe airplanes like some of the others, and I hated alert and the whole SAC mentality. Mostly, though, I was tired of being away from my family. I would go off TDY somewhere, and while I was gone my sons would learn to take their first steps or say their first words. I was missing seeing them grow up.

If I was going to get out at the end of five years, I had to give six months' written notice. There was also a very real chance I might be given orders to a different aircraft at any time. If that happened, I would be sent to another aircraft school and might end up with another three-year Air Force commitment. It had happened to other pilots I knew.

Ultimately, I put in my papers in December 1969 to get out of the Air Force on May 10, 1970. It was a good thing I did. In January, the whole Wing (bombers and tankers) received orders to move to the Island of Guam in the Pacific Ocean for six months of continuous Arc Light missions (B-52 bombing of Vietnam). I was not sorry to be left behind. By early May, Crew R-111 had been reassigned to someone else, but I volunteered to go out on one last refueling mission on May, 9 1970. Maj. Norm French, one of my former aircraft commanders, let me make the final landing that day. It was a piece of cake.

When it was finally over, I was somewhat surprised I had actually survived my Air Force career. Four men I knew well had not. Lt. Bill Causey never came back from his night training mission. Kindly old Colonel Bell, who certified me as a combat crewmember, bought the farm during a tanker heavy-weight takeoff at another base. Lt. Norm Bates had a midair collision in his light plane, and Capt. Leon Pierce's name is on "The Wall" in Washington, D. C. I did not know what my future held, but I was ready for a change.

My last day of active duty was bittersweet. I had to turn in my equipment, including my flight helmet and my twenty-four-hour wristwatch. I had to scrape my SAC identification sticker off of my car, and turn in my Air Force ID card. I was leaving some of the best friends I ever had. I was leaving an extremely prestigious profession and returning to the civilian world.

CHAPTER 14

CIVIL AVIATION

"I wonder what that P-3 Orion is doing over Alpine?"
Oscar Lopez, 1980s

After I left the Air Force, I completed the necessary paperwork and was licensed by the Federal Aviation Administration as a "Commercial Pilot, Airplane, Multi-engine, Land: Boeing 707/720 Aircraft with Instruments." Armed with my new commercial license, I applied to several airlines for a position as an airline pilot. However, May of 1970 was not a good time to be looking for an airline job. TWA (Trans World Airlines) laid off their first 200 pilots that month, and a lot of the other airlines soon followed suit. Some pilots I knew who got out of the Air Force six months ahead of me and got jobs as airline pilots were laid off that month and were still laid off three years later. I was glad I wasn't mixed up in that mess, and besides, one reason I had left the Air Force was to spend more time with my family, and an airline job wouldn't have solved that.

As it turned out, I never again flew as the pilot in command of an aircraft. However, I have had some interesting times as a wildlife biologist flying as a passenger on aerial wildlife surveys, photographic missions, habitat evaluations, and cross-country trips. Once we were safely airborne, most of the civilian pilots I knew would let me "stir the stick" a little, and I would sometimes fly for hours when we were going cross-country. Once we got down low, however, I always turned the flying back over to a pilot who did that kind of flying for a living. I noticed pretty quickly that flying through a narrow rocky canyon or bumping along only 100-200 feet above the ground counting waterfowl or deer is a lot different from flying through the stratosphere.

One of the more interesting flights I recall took place in far West Texas in the late 1980s. Oscar Lopez and I had flown out from Austin to the Ocotillo Wildlife Unit located on the Rio Grande about thirty miles upriver from Presidio. As we were coming into the dirt strip on top of a mesa that served as a landing field, I noticed polka dots all over the runway. Oscar explained it was just cow patties from free-ranging livestock. Oscar made a low approach to make sure there were no cows still on the runway and then came around and landed. When he touched down, dust and pebbles stirred up by the prop and the landing gear made a noise like shrapnel on the underside of the fuselage.

That was the first time I had been in an aircraft on a dirt strip in more than twenty years. We picked up another wildlife biologist and flew up and down the river for several miles, checking on flood damage to white-winged dove nesting habitat. Then we landed, picked up another biologist, and flew some more. By the time we got that done, it was getting very hot, and the air was getting thin.

When we lifted off that dirt strip the final time to head back to Alpine, the stall-warning horn started screaming and continued to scream for several minutes as Oscar very slowly and carefully circled over the Rio Grande floodplain to gain enough airspeed and altitude to climb up Pinto Canyon past Chinati Peak.

We landed back at Alpine for lunch, and as we walked out to the car, we were surprised to see a U.S. Navy P-3 "Orion" make a low pass over the field. The Orion was a four-engine turboprop aircraft used by the Navy for long-distance submarine patrols. We couldn't imagine what it was doing at Alpine. However, when we came back from lunch and there were two U.S. Army "Cobra" helicopter gunships parked on either side of our Texas Parks and Wildlife aircraft, everything suddenly became clear.

The Orion had been using its powerful airborne radar to detect light aircraft running drugs across the Rio Grande from Mexico. All of our circling around and multiple landings on the dirt strip had made them suspicious, and they had called in the gunships to force us down if necessary. Once the gunship crews saw who we were, they just went to lunch too.

CHAPTER 15

THE HOT AIR BALLOON RIDE

"I am a former Air Force test pilot.
I have been to 87,000 feet.
I have seen the blackness of space
and the curvature of the Earth,
but you wouldn't get me up
in a hot air balloon."
Lt. Col. Howard Kidwell, USAF, Ret.

Pilots always enjoy watching aircraft, and for several years while we were living in Iowa, the National Hot Air Balloon Championships were held in Indianola, not far from our home. I got a kick out of watching the multicolored balloons drifting by slowly overhead. Even after we moved back to Texas, we would occasionally see hot air balloons drifting around Austin, and I apparently remarked once too often to Barbara that those balloons looked like fun. At any rate, when I opened my Christmas present one year, it was a gift certificate from Barb that said, "Good for one hot air balloon ride within 90 days."

Well, I called up and scheduled a balloon ride for February 11, 1990. I was supposed to meet the balloon driver, a guy named "Terry" in Zilker Park on Town Lake in downtown Austin. Sure enough, Terry was there when we got there, and he and his ground crew were dragging a beautiful multicolored balloon, a basket, burners, fan, and other stuff out of a pickup truck.

Bystanders were helping out, and for some reason, this scene reminded me of old movies about biplanes and barnstormers in the 1920s. Terry introduced me to my fellow balloon travelers, a couple of tiny little old ladies. Terry said we would be taking off as soon as we got the balloon inflated.

First, the ground crew spread the balloon out on the ground. Then they used a gasoline-powered fan to partially inflate the balloon. Next, they lit the propane burners and filled the balloon with hot air. As the hot air in the balloon began to rise, the balloon became more and more erect until it was standing completely upright with the basket attached by ropes to the bottom of the balloon. The crew and various bystanders were holding on to ropes and the basket to keep the balloon from drifting off. Terry helped the little old ladies into the basket and then invited me to climb in.

The sides of the wicker basket were about four and a half feet tall in the corners where it attached to metal uprights, but the basket dipped down so low between the corners I could step over the side about midpoint. This did not look like a very safe arrangement to me! We didn't have safety harnesses, parachutes, or anything. I backed up and wedged myself into one corner, got a death grip on a metal upright with one hand, and clawed my fingers into the other side of the basket.

Terry fired the burner again and told the rope holders to cast off. We lifted smoothly and rapidly almost straight up like an elevator in the sky. Terry got out a hand-held radio, contacted Aircraft Departure Control at Robert Mueller Municipal Airport, and told them he was a balloon launching from Zilker Park and he was "Headed south, apparently." Departure Control acknowledged his transmission, and that was the last we heard from them.

The balloon continued to rise almost straight up and eventually reached an indicated altitude of 3,500 feet (about 3,000 above the ground). The little old ladies were having a ball peering over the side of the basket. I was not. I was too tall for this particular basket. It looked to me like I would go right over the side if I happened to slip. In addition, since there was no sensation of forward airspeed, I had the feeling we were stalled. Based on all of my flying experience, any aircraft that is stalled is about to go down. This was a very unpleasant sensation.

Terry must have noticed I looked a little tense because he asked me if I was all right. I explained my uneasiness and my previous flying experience. Terry said not to worry, the basket was perfectly safe and promptly demonstrated by jumping up and down on the wooden floor and rocking the basket side to side. I could have killed him!

Periodically, Terry would lean over the side and spit to judge his forward progress. He never held on to anything, but he was shorter than I was, and maybe he felt like most of his center of gravity was safely inside the basket.

I noticed right away we could hear everything on the ground. The huge expanse of the Earth served as a reflector for any noises from below. We could clearly hear people talking far below us, and we could hear every dog in South Austin barking every time Terry lit the burners.

Terry told us he could usually expect winds from slightly different directions at different altitudes, and by climbing or descending he could steer the balloon to some degree. Unfortunately, there was so little wind at any altitude that day, he could not steer effectively.

We continued to drift slowly southward toward the big parking lot at Toney Burger Center. Terry tried to land there but couldn't quite make the balloon go that direction. By now, we were past the open areas and drifting over residential areas in South Austin which were dominated by large live oak trees. Terry saw an open area and began to descend. As we got closer, we could see an animal running back and forth across the opening. Closer inspection revealed the animal was a huge Doberman pinscher, and it was barking hysterically and hitting the fence time after time in an effort to get at us. Terry said we probably wouldn't land there.

Terry continued his descent, though, and soon our basket was just skimming the tops of the live oak trees by maybe ten feet or so. For me, this was the most enjoyable part of the ride. It was like riding a magic carpet! Terry had amazing altitude control, and he added burners as needed to raise us up over the tops of the taller trees and then let us settle down into the valleys. On and on we went over seemingly endless treetops.

All of a sudden, a voice rose up out of the trees and said, "You better not want to land that thing here." We peered down among the branches and saw an old man grubbing around in the dirt in a hog pen, and Terry said, "No, sir!"

We climbed a little bit and eventually came to a street with

two potential landing sites: a front yard and a garden divided by
a tall powerline. Terry hollered at two girls about ten years old
who were walking along the street and said, "Is it okay for us to
land in your yard?" The girls looked up, but they were so surprised they didn't know what to say.

Fortunately, a man came out of the house, realized what was
happening, and said, "Come on down." Terry tried to land in
the front yard, but the wind blew us back over the powerlines.
For several seconds we just hung over the powerlines then drift-
ed slowly over the garden. As soon as Terry judged he was clear
of the powerlines, he pulled a line and dumped part of our
canopy. The balloon descended rapidly about seventy-five feet
straight down, and I could tell the basket was going to land
exactly in the top of a big peach tree. When we hit the tree, we
tore off a big limb and tilted over in the basket. Terry dumped
the rest of our hot air, and the balloon came down limply and
deflated onto the ground.

Residents of the neighborhood had surrounded us, and
Terry was apologizing for the peach tree. However, these people
didn't care; they were just thrilled to have a hot air balloon land
in their yard! After we got everything gathered up and placed in
the chase vehicle, Terry brought out a bottle of champagne, and
we all toasted our successful flight.

It had certainly been an interesting afternoon, but I think
it cured me of wanting another hot air balloon ride any time
soon.

CHAPTER 16

THE 20TH YEAR REUNION

Question: "How do you know if there's a fighter
pilot at your party?"
Answer: "He will tell you."

In 1986, Ron Bandsuch, Jim Cross, and I co-hosted the 20th Year Reunion of Pilot Training Class 66-G from Webb Air Force Base, Texas. We held the reunion at the Hyatt Regency Hotel in Austin. Eleven of our twenty-one classmates were able to make the reunion. Ed King had died of leukemia, and we had lost Bill Causey in the B-52 accident, but no one else had been killed or injured in a military aircraft. That was remarkable, considering we graduated in 1966 just as the Vietnam Conflict was heating up, and many of us had flown combat missions.

I had not seen most of my classmates since the day we graduated. Some had changed remarkably, others hardly at all. There was Captain (now Colonel) Bill Stocker, our former class commander. He had flown over 300 combat missions in Southeast Asia in bomber aircraft. He had led the first B-52 strike against heavily defended targets around Hanoi, where we lost so many planes. Bill's hair had turned snow white.

David Bean had flown more than 370 combat missions in F-4 fighters. His chest was covered with decorations for valor, but that former hell-raiser we had known was now a quiet, modest, born-again Christian.

Bob Kusterer, a licensed "Stearman" biplane pilot and an

aeronautical engineer before he went to Air Force pilot training (and one of the top men in our class), was now an American Airlines pilot and F-106 fighter-interceptor pilot with the Massachusetts Air National Guard. Kusterer had photographs of his aircraft intercepting a Soviet TU-20 "Bear" (a four-engine nuclear bomber with counter-rotating props) just off the New England coast. Kusterer flew an F-106 nonstop from Massachusetts, with just a single in-flight refueling, to the "Aerofest" air show at Bergstrom AFB to be at our reunion.

Jim Cross from Cumby, Texas, with whom I had gone through both college and pilot training, had flown light planes as a forward air controller marking enemy targets with smoke rockets. He had seen the Vietnam Conflict up close and personal.

Ron Bandsuch, we found out, lived less than twenty miles from us just outside of Austin. Ron had flown C-130 "Hercules" cargo planes all over the world and had recently switched to the huge C-5 cargo plane. Ron remained in the service longer than any of the rest of us and ultimately flew more than thirty missions to Saudi Arabia supplying American troops during "Desert Storm."

Len Bara had been a T-37 instructor pilot at Wichita Falls. John Ball, Taylor Eubank, Bob Whitcomb, Paul "Tiger" Tiley, and Fithian Shaw (from another section of the class) had all been F-4 fighter jocks at various places around the world. One of our old instructor pilots from Webb AFB, Capt. James Finfinger, also attended the reunion.

It was great to see all of them and to reminisce about all of our flying experiences. Other than family, I felt closer to those men than any other bunch of guys I have ever known.

About the Author

Former U.S. Air Force Captain Ron George is the middle of three brothers who all became Air Force officers. He grew up on the family farm and cattle ranch near Greenville, Texas.

Ron received a B.S. degree in general science at East Texas State University and was commissioned a second lieutenant in the Air Force in 1965. He flew T-37 and T-38 aircraft during pilot training at Webb Air Force Base, Texas (near Big Spring), and was trained as a KC-135 jet tanker copilot at Castle AFB, California. His permanent duty station with the Strategic Air Command (SAC) was at Dyess AFB, Texas (near Abilene), where he and his aircrew pulled alert duty in the Mole Hole. Temporary duty trips took them to Alaska, Greenland, Newfoundland, Okinawa, and Southeast Asia.

Ron and his crew logged more than 200 hours of combat air time in their unarmed aircraft refueling American fighters and bombers striking targets in North Vietnam. They witnessed the communist "Tet Offensive" in South Vietnam in 1968 and participated in the "*Pueblo* Incident" in Korea.

When Ron upgraded to aircraft commander, he was thought to be the youngest aircraft commander in SAC since World War II. His military decorations include the Air Medal, the Vietnam Service Medal, and the Armed Forces Expeditionary Medal.

Ron left the Air Force in 1970 and completed an M.S. degree at Texas Tech University in range and wildlife science. For nearly thirty years he has served as a wildlife biologist, in Iowa and later in Texas. He is a Past-President of the Texas Chapter of The Wildlife Society. He is the chairman of the Migratory, Shore, and Upland Game Bird Subcommittee of the International Association of Fish and Wildlife Agencies and has been an invited guest lecturer on wildlife management in the People's Republic of China. He currently serves as the deputy director of the Wildlife Division and coordinator of wildlife research for Texas Parks and Wildlife.

Ron was selected as the Outstanding Alumnus of the Department of Range and Wildlife Management at Texas Tech University in 1988 and a Distinguished Alumnus of the College of Agriculture and Natural Sciences at Texas Tech University in 2000.

He is the author or co-author of more than sixty publications on wildlife conservation. This is his first book about his unique personal adventures. He and his wife, Barbara, live in Austin, Texas.